THE FOREST PASSAGE

THE FOREST PASSAGE

Ernst Jünger

Translated by Thomas Friese

Edited and with an Introduction by Russell A. Berman

Telos Press Publishing
Candor, NY

Printed in the United States of America
17   16   15   14   13   1   2   3   4

Translated by permission from the German original, *Der Waldgang*,
in Ernst Jünger, *Sämtliche Werke*, vol. 7, pp. 281–374, Stuttgart
1980. © 1951, 1980 Klett-Cotta—J. G. Cotta'sche Buchhandlung
Nachfolger GmbH, Stuttgart.

ISBN: 978-0-914386-49-0

Library of Congress Cataloging-in-Publication Data

Jünger, Ernst, 1895–1998.
   [Waldgang. English]
   The Forest Passage / Ernst Jünger ; translated by Thomas Friese ;
edited and with an introduction by Russell A. Berman.
      pages cm
   ISBN 978-0-914386-49-0
   I. Friese, Thomas. II. Title.
   PT2619.U43W313 2013
   838'.91209—dc23

                                          2013039459

Telos Press Publishing
PO Box 811
Candor, NY 13743

www.telospress.com

Contents

Translator's Preface

Thomas Friese

"I would not encourage in your minds that delusion which you must carefully foster in the minds of your human victims. I mean the delusion that the fate of nations is in itself more important than that of individual souls. The overthrow of free peoples and the multiplication of slave-states are for us a means...; the real end is the destruction of individual souls. For only individuals can be saved or damned..."

C. S. Lewis, *The Screwtape Letters*

These words from Screwtape's toast to young devils graduating from Hell's training college describe—more or less precisely, if the religious concepts are set aside—the subject of this key Jüngerian work: it is the timeless theme of the salvation of the individual in the world, here in the contemporary context of globalization, technically all-powerful and manipulative states, and disintegrating support institutions such as family and church.

The salvation that may be found "in the forest" is understood, above all, as the preservation, or recovery, of the individual's freedom, psychological and concrete, in the face of materially superior forces intent on imprisoning him—by violence, intimidation, or propaganda—and exploiting or destroying him for their own gain. This individual return to a primal relation with freedom in the midst of collective slavery Jünger calls the forest passage. And, as the forces seeking to exploit man today are but the latest incarnations of forces that have threatened individual freedom throughout history, so the path he sets down for the forest rebel is his recasting of ways that philosophers, religions, and esoteric movements prepared for past historical and spiritual human predicaments. In Jünger's version it is a self-empowered initiative, reliant on no external institutions, which in our present reality are non-existent or fundamentally bankrupt. It is a path that takes strength and guidance from more basic and indestructible human factors, such as friendship, love, or conscience, and it is to be discovered and blazed by the individual in the "here and now" of his worldly experience.

While a forest passage may bring collateral benefits for society, in particular for other individuals, it does not aim primarily at world-improvement: the collective, as a whole, is essentially beyond redemption, *a priori* a lost cause. It is only individuals, forest rebels within society, that can hope, as exceptions, to escape the coercion, to "save their own souls." The forest rebel battles the Leviathan not in the hopes of defeating it—for it eventually collapses under its own enormous weight—though he may promote this inevitable demise by inflicting strategic damage on it, and he can already help define and introduce the seeds of new freedoms for a post-Leviathan world. Rather, the forest rebel has two other immediate motivations in the here and now: first, to save himself (before trying to help a neighbor in the catastrophe, as parents are told to put on their own oxygen masks in an airplane crash before those of their children); and second, and not unrelated, to obey his conscience, the directives of an intact and normal humanity, which feels natural concern for its fellow human beings.

Jünger and the forest rebel represent no specific political agenda here, for the oppression to be resisted at all costs may be openly manifested in tyrannies or cunningly disguised in democracies, and it may arrive from the east or the west. In a certain sense his vision is even democratic, for the forest passage is available always and to everyone, regardless of their political, social, geographic, or economic reality. However, it is also anything but egalitarian and it is not a realistic option for the masses, for it presupposes a great inner distancing from society, an extraordinary strength of will, and uncommon courage.

Since the publication of *Eumeswil* (1977), no discussion of the forest rebel can be complete without mention of its successor in that later work, the anarch, in my opinion Jünger's crowning achievement. Indeed, all the qualities ascribed to the forest rebel in *The Forest Passage* are present in the anarch, and then some, for the anarch is his stronger twin, comprehending all that he is and taking the development further. The two figures may differ in degrees of personal power and freedom, but essentially, or existentially, they are almost identical, and a forest passage always remains for the anarch as one in a set of contingent tactics:

> The forest flight confirms the independence of the anarch, who is basically a forest fleer anywhere, any time, whether in the thicket, in the metropolis, whether inside or outside society.[1]

> The forest fleer and the partisan are not, as I have said, to be confused with each other; the partisan fights in society, the forest fleer alone. Nor, on the other hand, is the forest fleer to be confused with the anarch, although the two of them grow very similar for a while and are barely to be distinguished in existential terms. The difference is that the forest fleer has been expelled from society, while the anarch has expelled society from himself.... When he [the anarch] decides to flee to the forest, his decision is less an issue of

---

1. Ernst Jünger, *Eumeswil*, trans. Joachim Neugroschel (New York: Marsilio Publishers, 1993), pp. 145–46.

justice and conscience for him than a traffic accident. He changes camouflage; of course, his alien status is more obvious in the forest flight, thereby making it the weaker form, though perhaps indispensable.[2]

I will make no attempt here to present the subtle differences between the two figures—the interested reader does best to pick up a copy of *Eumeswil* and form his own conclusions. But I will suggest that the ultimate importance of the present book lies precisely here: as preparatory material for a study of the anarch in *Eumeswil*. It then also goes without saying that the existence of *Eumeswil* and the anarch should not be understood as a reason to skip the earlier phase of the development and jump to the final product: as we saw above, Jünger himself reaffirmed the validity of the forest rebel in *Eumeswil*. Speaking also from personal experience, I encountered *Eumeswil* years before *The Forest Passage*—in Florence, Italy, through the excellent salons of the Association Eumeswil—and although we studied *Eumeswil* in depth, I did not fully understand its comments on the forest rebel until doing this translation. More importantly, by understanding the forest rebel I have gained a deeper and more grounded understanding of the anarch. The two figures are indeed best studied and understood together.

A final note regarding the translation of the book's title and protagonist, of the act and the actor. We saw above that the translator of *Eumeswil*, Joachim Neugroschel, translated "Waldgang" and "Waldgänger" as "forest flight" and "forest fleer." To be sure, these English terms have a catchy ring, form a convenient pair, and do reflect the internal and, when necessary, external distancing from society. Nevertheless, I departed from them, primarily because the word "flight" has a connotation of running away from normal reality, the choice

2. Ibid., p. 147.

of a weaker, not a stronger, individual. Naturally, the forest rebel does seek to escape oppression, and, being comparatively weaker than the anarch, he must "flee" society to some extent, while the anarch can remain concealed and wholly within it. However, the terms of comparison at the time Jünger conceived the figure of the *Waldgänger* were not the as-yet unborn anarch and his qualities, but the masses, and political activists, anarchists, and partisans. In comparison with these, the inner and outer positions the *Waldgänger* occupies require a stronger will, courage, and inner force; in this context, I find "flight," as reflecting a relative weakness, inappropriate.

Moreover, there is the dual sense of "Waldgang" in German: it can denote both a going to the forest and a walking or being in the forest, and both are implicit in Jünger's metaphor, which concerns moving to the new position *and* the state of being there. "Passage" reflects this dual character somewhat better than "flight," which focuses only on the going there, and, again, implies a weakness that is only such in relation to the even more exceptional figure of the anarch.

For the actor's name, I chose a compromise between Neugroschel's "forest fleer," which retains "forest," and the French and Italian translators who simply used "rebel," which this figure certainly also is. In this manner, a new term, the forest rebel, has also been coined for this freshly conceived and yet timeless existential figure of Ernst Jünger's.

INTRODUCTION

Russell A. Berman

Ernst Jünger's *The Forest Passage* is a call for resistance. It maps a strategy of opposition to oppressive power. Undertaking the forest passage means entering an anarchic realm beyond the control of the seemingly omnipotent state, while setting oneself apart from the masses who sheepishly obey the rulers' commands. The few who can tap the inner strength to fight back become "forest rebels," partisans pursuing freedom against unconstrained power.

The Forest Passage is the third in a series of Jünger texts published by Telos Press. In the earliest, *On Pain* (1934), Jünger reflects on transformations in warfare and on how they have changed traditional notions of subjectivity. It belongs to the important group of Jünger's writings marked by the battle-field experience in the First World War, but it also exemplifies his advocacy for the Conservative Revolution, the radical cultural opposition to Germany's Weimar Republic. This early phase in Jünger's work, especially his *Storm of Steel* (1920), has largely defined his reception, especially in the English-speaking world. In contrast, the second Telos Press volume, *The Adventurous Heart* (1938), shows Jünger's surrealist sensibility, an exploration of the grotesque and magic elements in everyday life and the subversion of normalcy as central to the modern experience. This disruption of rational order becomes his aesthetic project.

The Forest Passage (1951) documents a further chapter in Jünger's thought. It describes the urgency for a heroic elite to upset the machinery of total control. His resonant plea to push back against a constantly expansive bureaucratic power with unlimited capacities for surveillance makes *The Forest Passage* particularly timely today. It is a call to subvert the "Leviathan," the name Jünger gives the oppressive state, borrowed from the seventeenth-century political philosopher Thomas Hobbes.

Writing against the backdrop of the Nazi dictatorship, only recently defeated, and the contemporary spread of Soviet power throughout Eastern Europe, Jünger opens *The Forest Passage* by dissecting the manipulation inherent in fraudulent elections. Staged to demonstrate popular support, they are in fact mechanisms to control and suppress public opinion. To use Noam Chomsky's term, they "manufacture consent," since most of the public cooperates passively, automatically, and uncritically. As an alternative, Jünger invokes the possibility of resistance, even if only very few are likely to rise to the occasion. Despite massive police power, isolated rebels or small groups fight back against the manipulated order of the monstrous state. This is the new battlefield: "The armor of the new Leviathans has its own weak points, which must continually be felt out, and this assumes both caution and daring of a previously unknown quality. We may imagine an elite opening this battle for a new freedom, a battle that will demand great sacrifices and which should leave no room for any interpretations that are unworthy of it." The military terminology—the imagery of battle, the necessity of sacrifice, and the strategic identification of weak points—recalls Jünger's World War I texts. More than three decades later, he remains the soldier.

In *The Forest Passage*, however, the warrior goes beyond the description of the battlefield experience that marked the early writings in order to pursue a distinctive goal, Jünger's "new freedom." If it is striking to find the former conservative revolutionary appealing to freedom, the key is in the adjective "new." What sort of freedom does he mean? At stake is not the familiar enlightenment notion of individual autonomy; this is not business-as-usual liberalism. Such an understanding would be one of the "unworthy" interpretations to which he refers. On the contrary, Jünger explains by underscoring the gravity of the topic: "To find good comparisons we need to look back to the gravest of times and places—for instance to the Huguenots, or to the Guerrillas as Goya pictured them in his *Desastres*. By contrast, the storm of the Bastille, which still nourishes the awareness of individual freedom today, was a Sunday walk in the park." The contrast is instructive: religious wars and guerillas on the one hand, the storming of the Bastille on the other. It is a characteristic distinction for Jünger, but it needs to be decoded. The storming of the Bastille—that stands for the French Revolution, the representative symbol of the French Republic, the Declaration of the Rights of Man, and the centrist tradition of liberal thought. As an icon it depends on an optimistic view of human nature, a sanguine belief in progress and confidence in the rule of reason. For Jünger such complacent trust in the goodness of the friendly state is an illusion, and the fight at the Bastille little more than child's play, in contrast to the "gravest" scenes he conjures up with their much darker brutality. The persecution of the Huguenots reminds us of how religious freedom emerges from murderous violence and torture, just as the destructiveness of the wars in Spain in the Napoleonic era, the horrors of which Goya documented, was the price of national freedom. Religion—not enlightenment rationality—defines Jünger's account of freedom, as does myth, including the myth of the guerilla fighter, or the partisan, which Jünger shared with Carl Schmitt, whose *Theory of the Partisan* has also been published by Telos Press.

The Forest Passage charts a campaign for existential freedom: "The forest rebel thus possesses a primal relationship to freedom, which, in the perspective of our times, is expressed in his intention to oppose the automatism and not to draw its ethical conclusion, which is fatalism." The reference to "automatism" poses the question of technology. In Jünger's earlier writings, especially from the 1920s and 1930s, he explores two archetypes, the soldier and the worker, each of whom faces technology (albeit in different ways), which in turn transforms them both. By internalizing technology, they become machine-like and therefore come to stand for alternatives to cozy liberal understandings of subjectivity. In *The Forest Passage*, technology again looms large, but its impact is very different. For Jünger's soldier and worker, the assimilation of technology produced versions of the modernist utopia of a "new man." In contrast, the forest rebel faces technology in order to resist it because its "automatism" now turns out to amount to a degradation of human life. The enlightenment legacy of autonomy leads to this automatic behavior, a metamorphosis into an automaton, a robot. In contrast, the forest rebel searches for a qualitatively different outcome, a better alternative equal to humanity's capacity for freedom.

Meanwhile however the Leviathan imposes its stultifying order through threats and manipulation. The irrevocable dictates of the machine—be it the machinery of warfare or the machinery of politics—spread terror and fear. If one dares to stand out from the crowd, one risks punishment by the states' henchmen, gangsters in or out of uniform. "Where the automatism increases to the point of approaching perfection—such as in America—the panic is even further intensified. There it finds its best feeding grounds; and it is propagated through networks that operate at the speed of light. The need to hear the news several times a day is already a sign of fear; the imagination grows and paralyzes itself in a rising vortex. The myriad antennae rising above our megacities resemble hairs standing on end—they provoke demonic contacts." Insightful cultural observation is Jünger's forte. The unstoppable regularity of automatic machinery defines a cruelly enforced normalcy, which elicits fear, rather than the security it vainly promises. Or rather: the security state is itself replete with fear. A widespread response to this underlying existential anxiety is the neurotic need to listen to the news constantly, the bedtime story that the state broadcasts every hour to reassure the population that its narrative remains intact. Nonetheless fears of imagined enemies proliferate, eradicating vestiges of common sense. The image of the communications antennae resembling "hairs standing on end" as a symptom of fear stages a transition between biological organism and mechanical device. This human mimesis of machine existence draws on Jünger's longstanding concern with the metamorphic impact of machines on the human condition. Yet we do not have to become machines, as little as we have to live in fear. In *The Forest Passage* Jünger maps out the fight against mechanization and the potential for victory: "The chains of technology can be broken—and it is the individual that has this power."

As far as the individual is concerned, Jünger's topic is not that enlightenment subject at home in a world of rationality and consensus, who feels most comfortable with the abstractions of theory or claims about universal values. On the contrary, that sort of idealism turns out to have a deeply inhuman quality, as Jünger brilliantly points out when he writes that "we cannot limit ourselves to knowing what is good and true on the top floors while fellow human beings are being flayed alive in the cellar." The reality of the torture chamber undermines the very credibility of lofty norms, the "good and true," a hardly subtle reference to the specific tradition of German idealism and Kantian ethics. Six years after the collapse of the Nazi regime, Jünger takes on the paradox of Germany's two sides, the idealist legacy and the murderous history, high culture and horrific crime. After the cellars of the Gestapo and the concentration camps, it is impossible to accept the fairy tales about innate reason or the goodness of humanity.

Instead of that idealism, Jünger ascribes to the forest rebel a different, existential knowledge of the human condition. "[Freedom] is prefigured in myth and in religions, and it always returns; so, too, the giants and the titans always manifest with the same apparent superiority. The free man brings them down; and he need not always be a prince or a Hercules. A stone from a shepherd's sling, a flag raised by a virgin, and a crossbow have already proven sufficient." The examples are programmatic: the young David from the Hebrew Bible, felling the giant Goliath; Joan of Arc leading a nation in the name of God; and William Tell the sharpshooter and forest rebel, challenging the intrusive, bureaucratic state. None of these figures is a "prince." The elite to which they belong is not inherited; they display a heroism in their nature, not their pedigree, and they bring down tyrants through combinations of religion and patriotism. Their loyalty is not to the state but to much more profound forces.

The shepherd, the virgin, the archer—Jünger the aesthete has chosen literary examples. In addition, however, he also directs attention to two historical figures as representatives of rebellion. His choices are stunning: Petter Moen, a member of the Norwegian anti-Nazi resistance, tortured by the Gestapo, and Helmuth James Graf von Moltke, scion of a distinguished German military family who, because of his opposition to Hitler, was convicted of treason and executed. Jünger served as an officer in the German army in both world wars, so his focus on these two anti-Nazi heroes is indicative of his own contrarian thinking. Both were also writers. Von Moltke in his letters and Moen in his prison diary (written with a pin on toilet paper and hidden in his cell until it was discovered posthumously) provide testimonies to their individual integrity as well as their internal struggles. Their explicit invocation of religion, their moral inspiration, and their unwillingness to compromise provide important evidence as to the meaning of the forest passage. They also give us political coordinates to better understand the forest rebellion: the rebel maintains an uncompromising integrity, drawing on personal strength and the power of faith, to resist the brutality of the regime.

Religion is important for Jünger because it taps into dimensions of irrationality and myth, the deep wisdom at home in the forest. It is not that Jünger proselytizes or engages in theological speculation, but he recognizes how irrational contents nourish the capacity for independence. No wonder the regimes of power celebrate the cult of reason instead. "How is man to be prepared for paths that lead into darkness and the unknown? The fulfillment of this task belongs chiefly to the churches, and in many known, and many more unknown, cases, it has effectively been accomplished. It has been confirmed that greater force can be preserved in churches and sects than in what are today called worldviews—which usually means natural science raised to the level of philosophical conviction. It is for this reason that we see tyrannical regimes so rabidly persecuting such harmless creatures as the Jehovah's Witnesses—the same tyrannies that reserve seats of honor for their nuclear physicists." It is worth noting how the two twin totalitarianisms of the twentieth century each posed as the carrier of a scientific mission: the biological racism of Nazism and the economic "science of Marxism-Leninism" in Communism. From our contemporary point of view, of course, neither is a science, but Jünger's point is that modes of scientistic thinking are fully compatible with reigns of terror, while the integrity of faith may preserve a space of freedom, a leap of faith into the forest passage.

The complicity of science and technology in the administrative apparatus of control rings particularly true in our era of expansive surveillance and data collection. Jünger proves prescient on this point, particularly with regard to "the constantly increasing influence that the state is beginning to have on health services, usually under philanthropic pretexts." In *The Forest Passage*, Jünger gestures toward what would later come to be called biopolitics, the strategies of the state to manage and control its population through medical practices and technologies. "Given the widespread release of doctors from their doctor-patient confidentiality obligations, a general mistrust is also advisable for consultations; it is impossible to know which statistics one will be included in—also beyond the health sector. All these healthcare enterprises, with poorly paid doctors on salaries, whose treatments are supervised by bureaucracies, should be regarded with suspicion; overnight they can undergo alarming transformations, and not just in the event of war. It is not inconceivable that the flawlessly maintained files will then furnish the documents needed to intern, castrate, or liquidate." Jünger describes a world of intrusive government control, penetrating into previously private matters and increasingly limiting the individual's realm of freedom. The forest passage is the name he gives to the strategies to evade this Leviathan and to do battle with it.

Where does the forest rebel find the strength to oppose the overwhelming apparatus of the regime? Whether the regime relies on the direct violence of terroristic force or on the systematic propaganda of a culture industry or, more subtly, on the peer pressure of conformism, the rebel can offer resistance by mustering a personal integrity that draws on the deep wellsprings of human freedom, self-respect, and tradition. This is nowhere clearer than when Jünger asks why there was so little resistance in Germany to the state-sanctioned violence in

1933 and during the following years. His answer gets to the core of the anarchic forest rebel.

Once the Nazis came to power, they could use the apparatus of the modern state, with its unchecked authority, to invade the private sphere in ways impossible in earlier eras: "An assault on the inviolability, on the sacredness of the home, would have been impossible in old Iceland in the way it was carried out in 1933, among a million inhabitants of Berlin, as a purely administrative measure." No doubt Jünger romanticizes "old Iceland," but his point is that the modern administrative state lays claim to unlimited powers at odds with traditional notions of one's home as one's castle. To underscore his point, he offers a counterexample, an exceptional moment of resistance: "A laudable exception deserves mention here, that of a young social democrat who shot down half a dozen so-called auxiliary policemen at the entrance of his apartment. He still partook of the substance of the old Germanic freedom, which his enemies only celebrated in theory. Naturally, he did not get this from his party's manifesto—and he was certainly also not of the type Léon Bloy describes as running to their lawyer while their mother is being raped."

The extraordinary passage needs some parsing. The "so-called auxiliary policeman" were Nazi Storm Troopers, dubiously empowered (i.e., "so-called") to carry out police functions, in this case, to round up regime opponents. These Nazis had an ideological commitment to "Germanic" values, which however remained exclusively ideological, since they celebrated them only in theory, without trying to realize them in their lives. It was however the young Social Democrat who surpassed mere theory in order to put "the old Germanic freedom" into practice by resorting to violence. His alternative was to be led quietly to a concentration camp. When he resisted arrest, according to Jünger, he was not only a better German;

he was also more "Germanic," acting in accordance with an archaic notion of integrity. In any case, however, when he fought back, he was not following "his party's manifesto," since the Social Democrats would have condemned illegal or violent tactics. (Walter Benjamin makes an analogous criticism of Social Democratic passivity in his "Theses on the Philosophy of History" of 1940.) Léon Bloy's characteristically polemical remark underscores the point that there are situations of immediate violence and existential threat where formal reliance on legal procedure is as ineffectual as party manifestoes or theoretical allegiances. In this spirit, Jünger concludes that "the inviolability of the home" depends less on constitutions than on "the family father, who, sons at his side, fills the doorway with an axe in the hand." A mythical connection links the archaic image of the axe-wielding father from Iceland with the brave Social Democratic resistance fighter in Berlin. "If we assume that we could have counted on just one such person in every street of Berlin, then things would have turned out very differently than they did."

Without a doubt, *The Forest Passage* reverberates with the experience of the Nazi era. Yet it is not only a historical document. The figure of the forest rebel is, for Jünger, an expression of the human potential to take dangerous risks in the name of freedom and to mount resistance against a seemingly overpowering state. The capacity to push back against enslavement is grounded in humanity's inextinguishable force of creativity. "[I]t is essential to know that every man is immortal and that there is eternal life in him, an unexplored and yet inhabited land, which, though he himself may deny its existence, no timely power can ever take from him." That anarchic land, the forest beyond the borders of the state, beyond surveillance and terror, is replete with resources indispensable for a life worthy of humans. *The Forest Passage* leads us into it.

THE FOREST PASSAGE

1

The forest passage—it is no jaunt that is concealed in this title. Rather, the reader should be prepared for a dangerous expedition, leading not merely beyond the blazed trails but also beyond the limits of his considerations.

A core question of our times is concerned, that is, a question that will in any event involve personal danger. To be sure, we discuss questions a great deal, as our fathers and grandfathers before us did. But what is termed a question in this sense has naturally changed considerably since their days. Are we sufficiently aware of this yet?

The times are scarcely over when such questions were understood as great enigmas, even as cosmic enigmas, and accompanied by an optimism that was confident of finding answers. Other questions were viewed rather as practical problems, women's rights for instance, or the social question in general. These problems too were considered resolvable, albeit less through research than by an evolution of society toward new orders and arrangements.

In the meantime the social question has been worked out in broad regions of our globe. The classless society has developed it into more of an element of foreign policy than anything else. Of course, this by no means implies that the issues themselves have thereby disappeared, as was believed in the first rapturous moments; instead, other even more burning questions have arisen. One such question will occupy us here.

2

Our reader will have learned from personal experience that the nature of questions themselves has changed. Today we are unremittingly approached by questioning powers, and these powers are not motivated solely by the ideal of increasing knowledge. In coming to us with their questions, they are not expecting us to contribute to objective truth, nor even to solve specific problems. They are interested not in our solutions but in our answers.

This is an important difference. It turns the questioning into something closer to an interrogation. This can be followed in the evolution from the electoral ballot to the questionnaire. An electoral ballot aims at purely numerical ratios and the evaluation thereof. It exists to fathom the will of the voters, and the voting procedure is designed to produce a pure representation of this will, unaffected by external influences. Voting is thus accompanied by the sense of security—and even power—that characterizes a freely expressed act of will within a legal sphere.

The contemporary man who sees himself prevailed upon to fill out a questionnaire is far from any such security. The answers he provides will have far-reaching consequences; his very fate often depends on them. We see people getting into predicaments where they are required to produce documents aimed at their own ruin—and what trifles may not cause ruin today.

It is apparent that this change in the nature of questioning presages a quite different order from what we had at the beginning of the century. The old sense of security is gone, and our thinking must be adjusted accordingly. The questions press in on us, more closely and insistently, and the way we answer becomes all the more significative. We also need to keep in mind that silence itself is an answer. They ask why we kept quiet at just that place and time, and present us the bill for our response. These are the quandaries of our times, which none can escape.

It is remarkable how under such conditions everything becomes an answer in this special sense, and thereby a matter of our responsibility. Thus, perhaps even today, we do not clearly enough perceive to what degree the electoral ballot has been transformed into a questionnaire. All those not lucky enough to live in some sheltered reserve already know this, inasmuch as their *actions* are concerned: in response to threat we always adjust our actions before our theories. Yet it is only through reflection that we gain new security.

Consequently, the voter we are considering here approaches the ballot box with a quite different feeling than his father or grandfather did. No doubt he would prefer to stay clear of it altogether, yet precisely that would be to express an unequivocal answer. On the other hand, if we take fingerprinting technology and cunning statistical methods into account, participation appears equally hazardous. Why then is he supposed to vote in a situation in which choice no longer exists?

The answer is that the electoral ballot provides our voter an opportunity to join in an act of approbation with his own contribution. Not all are deemed worthy of this privilege— indeed, the voting lists undoubtedly do not include the names of the unknown legion from which our modern slave armies are recruited. Our voter thus takes care to know what is expected of him.

So far things are clear. In step with the development of dictatorships, free elections are replaced by plebiscites. The scope of the plebiscites, however, reaches beyond the sectors previously encompassed by the elections. The election becomes much more another form of plebiscite.

Where the leaders or the symbols of the state are put on show, the plebiscite can take on a public character. The spectacle of great, passionately aroused masses is one of the most important signs of our entrance into a new era. Within these hypnotic spheres there reigns, if not unanimity, then certainly a single voice—because to raise a dissenting voice here would lead to uproar and the destruction of its owner. A single person seeking to make his presence felt in this manner might as well opt to attempt an assassination—it would lead to the same thing.

Where a plebiscite is disguised as a form of free election, however, a point will be made to emphasize its confidential nature. In this way, the dictatorship attempts to produce proof not only of its support by an enormous majority but also of an approval grounded in the free will of individuals. The art of leadership rests not simply in asking questions in the right manner but also in the overall orchestration, which is monopolistic. Its task is to present the event as an overwhelming chorus, one that arouses terror and veneration.

Thus far matters seem clear, though perhaps novel for an older observer. The voter finds himself faced with a question, and there are convincing grounds to recommend that he align his answer with the questioner's goals. However, the real difficulty for the questioner here is that an illusion of freedom must simultaneously be maintained. Therewith, as with every moral process in these spheres, the question leads into statistics. We will further examine these details—they lead to our theme.

3

From a technical perspective, elections in which a hundred percent of the votes are cast in the desired manner present no difficulties. This target was achieved from the start, even surpassed, since more votes than voters turned up in certain boroughs. Incidents like this point to mistakes in the orchestration, which not all populations can be expected to put up with. With subtler propagandists at the helm, the matter is as follows.

One hundred percent: the ideal number, and, like all ideals, eternally unreachable. But it can be approached, as in sports, where certain limits, even unattainable ones, are approached by fractions of seconds or meters. How close an approach is allowable is in turn itself a function of a wealth of intricate deliberations.

In places where a dictatorship is already firmly established, even a ninety percent affirmation would fall too far short. A secret enemy in every tenth person—this is a consideration that the masses cannot be asked to accept. On the other hand, a count of spoiled and nay votes around two percent would be not only tolerable but even favorable. Yet we will not write off these two percent as mere dead wood. They merit a closer look, for it is precisely in such residues that the unsuspected may be found today.

From the organizer's perspective these two votes have a double utility. In the first place, they validate the remaining ninety-eight percent of votes by showing that they too could have been cast as these two were. In this manner the endorsement gains value, is authenticated and fully validated. It is important for dictators to be able to show that the freedom to say no has not been extinguished under them. This attitude of theirs in fact conceals one of the greatest compliments that can be made to freedom.

The second benefit of our two percent consists in their sustaining the uninterrupted movement that dictatorships rely on. It is for this reason that they continue to insist on presenting themselves as a "party," though it is meaningless. With a hundred percent the ideal would be achieved—and this would bring with it the dangers associated with every consummation. Even the laurels of civil war can be rested on. At the sight of all large fraternal gatherings, the question must be asked: And where is the enemy? For such large fusions are at the same time exclusions—exclusions of a despised third party, who is nonetheless indispensable. Propaganda relies on a situation in which the state enemy, the class enemy, the enemy of the people has been thoroughly beaten down and made almost ridiculous, yet not altogether eliminated.

Dictatorships cannot survive on pure affirmation—they need hate, and with it terror, to provide a simultaneous counterbalance. With a hundred percent good votes the terror would become meaningless; one would encounter only the good and upright everywhere. This is the other significance of the two percent. They show that, although the good may be in the vast majority, they are not wholly out of danger. On the contrary, in view of such convincing unity it must be assumed that only an exceptional grade of impenitence can hold itself apart. These must be saboteurs of the ballot—and does it not then also stand to reason that they will progress to other kinds of sabotage when the opportunity arises?

It is at this point that the electoral ballot becomes a questionnaire. It is unnecessary here to presume individual accountability for the supplied answers; yet we may be sure that numerical correlations exist. We may be certain that, by the logic of double-entry accounting, these two percent will reappear in other records than the election statistics, for instance in the registers of penitentiaries and penal labor camps, or in those places where God alone counts the victims.

This is the other function that this tiny minority performs for the vast majority—the first, as we saw, consisted in lending value, indeed reality, to the ninety-eight percent. But, even more importantly, no one wants to be reckoned among the two percent, in which a dark taboo makes itself visible. On the contrary, everyone will make a point of letting his good vote be broadly known. And should he indeed belong to the two percent, he will keep his vote secret from even his best friends.

A further benefit of this taboo consists in its action also against the category of non-voters. Non-participation is one of the attitudes that unsettles the Leviathan, though its potential is easily overestimated by outsiders. In the face of danger it quickly melts away. Near-perfect voter participation can therefore invariably be counted on, and the votes in favor of the questioner will scarcely be fewer.

For the voter it will be important to be seen at the voting station. To be absolutely safe, he will also let a few acquaintances see his ballot before he puts it into the box. Ideally, this favor is performed reciprocally, providing mutually dependent witnesses that the crosses went in the right places. A wealth of instructive variations exist here, which a good European who has never had the chance to study such situations would never dream of. Among the recurring figures there is thus always the upright citizen who hands in his ballot with the words: "Couldn't we just as well hand them in unfolded?" To which the electoral official responds, with a congenial, cryptic smile: "Yes, you're right—but we shouldn't really."

Visits to places like these sharpen the eye for studies of power questions. One homes in on one of the neural ganglia. However, it would lead too far afield to occupy ourselves here with the details of the arrangements. Let it suffice now to consider the singular figure of the man who enters such a place set on voting no.

4

Our man's *intention* may not be unique at all; it may be shared by many others, in all likelihood by significantly more than the mentioned two percent of the electorate. The orchestrators, by contrast, will try to dupe him into believing that he is very much alone. And not just that—the majority should impose itself not merely numerically but also through signs of moral superiority.

Let us assume that our voter, thanks to his powers of discrimination, has withstood the long, unambiguous propaganda campaign that has been astutely ramped up right until election day. This was no easy task. Now, on top of that, the statement required of him is clothed in highly respectable formulations: he is called on to participate in a vote for freedom, or perhaps a peace referendum. But who does not love peace and freedom? Only a monster. A nay vote already receives a criminal character here; and the bad voter resembles a criminal slinking up to the scene of a crime.

How invigorating, on the other hand, the day is for the good voter. During breakfast, he received final encouragement, his final instructions, over the radio. Now he goes into the street, where a festive mood prevails. Banners hang from every house and every window. He is welcomed in the courtyard of the electoral station by a band playing marches. The musicians are in uniform, and there is no lack of uniforms in the voting hall either. In his enthusiasm it will escape the good voter that one can hardly still talk of voting booths here.

On the other hand, it is precisely this circumstance that most absorbs the attention of the bad voter. He finds himself, pencil in hand, across from the electoral officials, whose presence disconcerts him. He makes his entry on a table that may, perhaps, still have the remnants of a green curtain around it. The arrangement has clearly been carefully thought through. It is unlikely that the point where he makes his cross can be seen; but can the opposite be altogether excluded? Just the day before he heard rumors that the ballot papers would receive numbers from ribbonless typewriters. At the same time, he wants to ensure that the next voter in line cannot peer over his shoulder. On the wall a giant portrait of the head of state, also uniformed, stares down at him with a frozen smile.

The ballot paper to which he now turns his attention also emanates suggestive power. It is the product of careful consideration. Under the words "Vote for Freedom" stands a large circle, with a superfluous arrow indicating: "Your Yes here." The small circle for No almost disappears next to it.

The big moment has arrived—our voter makes his entry. Let us put ourselves in spirit into his position: he has actually voted no. In reality, this act is a point of intersection of a series of fictions that we have yet to investigate: the election, the voter, the electoral posters are labels for quite other processes and things. They are picture puzzles. During their ascent dictatorships owe their survival in large part to the fact that their hieroglyphs have yet to be deciphered. Later they too find their Champollion—and while he may not bring back the old freedom, he does teach how to answer correctly.

It seems that our man has fallen into a trap. This makes his behavior no less admirable. Although his nay may issue from a lost cause, it will nevertheless have a persisting influence. Naturally, in places where the old world still basks in the warmth of the evening sun, on pleasant hillsides, on islands, or, in short, in milder climates, this voter will remain unnoticed. There it is the other ninety-eight of the hundred votes that make the impression. Since the cult of the majority has

been long and ever more mindlessly celebrated, the two percent will be overlooked. Their role, by contrast, is to make the
majority explicit and overpowering—because a hundred out
of a hundred can no longer be called a majority.

In countries where genuine elections still take place, such
success will at first elicit amazement, adulation, also envy. If
its impact extends into foreign affairs, these feelings may sour
into hate and contempt. Here the two righteous souls—unlike
with God and Sodom—will be overlooked. Opinions will circulate that all there have sworn themselves to the devil and are
ripe for a well-deserved fall.

5

Let us now put aside the ninety-eight percent and turn to the
residues, to the two grains of gold left in our sieve. To this end
we step through the locked door behind which the votes are
counted. Here we enter into one of the taboo zones of plebi-
scitary democracies, about which there exists only *one* official
view but numerous whispered ones.

The committee we meet here is also in uniform—though
perhaps in shirtsleeves—and exudes a spirit of familiar socia-
bility. It is composed of local representatives of the sole ruling
power, plus propaganda experts and police. The atmosphere is
that of a shopkeeper counting his take—not without suspense,
since all present in the room are more or less responsible for
the results. The yeas and nays are read out—the first with sym-
pathetic, the second with malignant satisfaction. Then come
the spoiled and empty ballots. The atmosphere becomes most
uncomfortable when the epigram of some joker pops up—certainly a rarity these days. Humor—together with the rest of
freedom's entourage—is absent in tyranny's sphere of influence; yet the wit is all the more cutting when the joker puts his
own head on the line.

Let us suppose that in the location we find ourselves the propaganda, with all its intimidating effects, has been developed to relatively high levels. In this case, rumors will circulate in the population that a large number of nay votes were turned into yeas. In all likelihood this was not even necessary. The opposite may even have transpired, in that the interrogator had to invent nays to reach the numbers he was reckoning with. What is certain is that he gives the law to the voters, and not they him. The dethronement of the masses that emerged during the twentieth century becomes apparent here.

Under these circumstances, finding only a *single* nay vote among the hundred in the box would already mean plenty. This vote's holder can be expected to make sacrifices for his convictions and his conception of freedom and right.

6

This vote—or rather, its holder—may also decide whether the constantly threatening condition of a termite state can be avoided. The accounts, which often seem so convincing to the spirit, will not work out at this spot, even if it is only a tiny fraction that remains over.

It is thus a true form of resistance that we meet here, though one that is still ignorant of its own strength and the manner in which this should be exerted. By making his cross on the dangerous spot, our voter does precisely what his vastly superior opponent expects of him. It is, without doubt, the act of a brave man, but so too an act of one of the countless illiterates in the new questions of power. This is someone who must be helped.

In sensing that he was falling into a trap in the polling station, our man correctly recognized his predicament. He was somewhere where the names no longer fit the things happening there. Above all, as we saw, it was no longer a ballot slip but a questionnaire that he filled out, and with that he was no longer in a free relation but was instead confronted by his authorities. By making his cross, as one voter in a hundred, on the nay spot, he merely contributed to the official statistics. While endangering himself out of all proportion, he provided the desired data to his opponent, for whom a hundred percent of the votes would have been far more unsettling.

But how should our man behave if he is to pass up the last possibility conceded him to express his views? With this question, we touch the borders of a new science—the teaching of human freedom in the face of changed forms of power. Though this will go far beyond our individual case here, let us pause to examine this case.

The voter finds himself faced with a real dilemma, since he is invited to make a free decision by a power that for its part has no intention of playing by the rules. This same power demands his allegiance, while it survives on breaches of allegiance. He is essentially depositing his honest capital in a crooked bank. Who can then reproach him if he plays along with the questionnaire and keeps his nay to himself? This is his right, not only for reasons of self-preservation, but also because such conduct can reveal a contempt for the ruling powers that is even superior to a nay.

This is not to say that our man's nay must be lost to the external world. On the contrary—it must only not appear at the location that the ruling powers have picked out for it. There are other places where it can makes things significantly more uncomfortable for these powers—on the white border of an electoral poster, for instance, on a public telephone book, or on the side of a bridge that thousands cross every day. A few words there, such as "I said no," would be far more effective.

Something else from our own personal experience should be shared with the young man whom we are advising: "Last week, in a local tractor factory, the word 'hunger' was discovered written on a wall. The workers were assembled and their pockets emptied. One of the pencils that were discovered had traces of whitewash on its point."

On the other hand, through the pressure they themselves create, dictatorships open up a series of weak points that simplify and condense the possibilities for attack. Sticking with our example, even the whole sentence above would not be necessary. A short "No" would suffice, because everyone whose eye it caught would know exactly what was meant. It would be a sign that the oppression had not entirely succeeded. Symbols stand out particularly well on monotoned backgrounds. The gray expanses correlate with a concentration into a minimized space.

The signs can manifest as colors, figures, or objects. Where they have an alphabetic character, the script is transformed into pictography. In the process, it gains immediate life, becomes hieroglyphic, and now, rather than explaining, it offers subject matter requiring explanation. One could further abbreviate and, in the place of "No," simply use a single letter—say, an R. This could indicate: Reflect, Reject, React, Rearm, Resist. It could also mean: Rebel.

This would be a first step out of the world of statistical surveillance and control. Yet the question at once arises if the individual is strong enough for such a venture.

7

There are two objections to consider at this point. The question could be raised if this single refusal registered on a ballot slip has any real meaning? On a higher moral plane such concerns have no place. A man expresses his view, in whichever forum it may be; he also accepts the possibility of downfall.

There can be no objection to this position, although expecting it in practice would amount to an extinction of the elite, and there have indeed been cases where it was required in bad faith. No, a vote like this cannot be lost, even if it issues from a lost cause. Precisely this status gives it special meaning. It will not shake the opponent, but it will change the person who has decided to go through with it. Until now he was one supporter of a political conviction among all the others—in the face of the new abuses of power, he is transformed into a combatant who makes a personal sacrifice, perhaps even into a martyr. This transformation is independent of the content of his conviction—when the confrontation arrives, the old systems and the old parties are transformed along with the rest. They are unable find the way back to their ancestral freedom. A democrat who has cast a solitary vote for democracy against ninety-nine others has thereby departed not only from his own political system but also from his individuality. This has repercussions reaching far beyond the passing process, since there can now be neither democracy nor the individual in the old sense.

This is why the numerous attempts under the Caesars to return to the republic had to fail. The republicans either fell in the civil war, or they came out of it transformed.

8

The second objection is still more difficult to rebut—and some readers will already have come to it: why should only the single nay carry weight? Is it not conceivable that among the ninety-nine other votes there may be some that were cast out of full, sincere conviction, and with good reasons?

In reality this is incontestable. We reach a point here at which any rapprochement seems impossible. The objection is valid, even if only a *single* genuine yea vote had been cast.

Let us consider an ideal yea and an ideal nay. The dichotomy that the times bring with them becomes manifest in the holders of these two votes; it raises its pro and contra in the breast of each individual too. The yea would stand for necessity, the nay for freedom. The historical process is such that both powers, necessity and freedom, act upon it. It degenerates when one of the two is missing.

Which of the two sides will be seen depends not only on the situation but above all on the observer. Nevertheless, he will always be able to sense the opposite side. He will be limited in his freedom by necessity, yet just through this freedom can he confer a characteristic style upon the necessary. This creates the gap by which men and peoples are either adequate to the times or are wrecked on them.

In the forest passage we consider the freedom of the individual in this world. An account must additionally be given of the difficulty—indeed of the merit—of managing to be an individual in this world. There can be no disputing that the world has changed and continues to change, and that by necessity; yet freedom thereby also changes, not in its essence but in its form. We live in the age of the Worker; since its conception this thesis can only have become more apparent. The forest passage establishes the movement within this order that differentiates it from zoological formations. Neither a liberal act nor a romantic one, it is rather the arena of a small elite, which knows what the times demand, and something more.

9

Our solitary voter is not yet a forest rebel. From a historical perspective he is even in arrears; his act of negation itself indicates this. Only when he has gained an overview of the game can he come up with his own, perhaps even surprising, moves.

To gain this vantage point he must first abandon the framework of the old majority conceptions, which continue to operate, despite having been thoroughly seen through by Burke and Rivarol. In that framework a minority of one percent is quite meaningless. As we saw, it simply serves to confirm the overwhelming majority.

This all changes the moment we abandon the statistics and turn to evaluative considerations. In this regard the solitary vote sets itself so far apart from all others that it even determines their market value. We may assume that this voter is not only capable of forming his own opinions, but that he also knows how to stand by them. Thus we can additionally concede our man courage. If there are still individuals to be found who are able, during long periods of the absolute dominion of violence, to preserve a notion of justice, even in the role of victim, then it is here that we must look. Even where they are silent, like submerged boulders in the stream they always generate a certain agitation in their vicinity. Their example shows that a predominating force, even one that changes history, is incapable of creating justice.

Viewing the matter from this angle, it appears that the power of an individual in the midst of the undifferentiated masses is not inconsiderable. One must remember that such an individual is almost always surrounded by others, whom he influences and who share in his fate if he falls. These others are also different from the members of a bourgeois family or from good friends from the past—stronger bonds are at work here.

The consequence is no longer merely the resistance of one in a hundred voters but of one in a hundred citizens. Though this calculation does have the flaw of including children, it is also true that in civil war people come of age, become responsible younger. Then again, the figure can also be set higher in lands that enjoy a venerable legal tradition. However, we are no longer dealing with numerical ratios here, but rather with a concentration of being, and with that we enter a different order. In this new order it makes no difference whether the voice of one individual contradicts a hundred or a thousand others. So too, his judgment, his will, and his effect can outweigh that of ten, twenty, or a thousand other men. The moment he decides to take the risk and abandon the realm of statistics, the senselessness of these pursuits, which lie far from the origins, will become clear to him.

Let it suffice us here to assume the existence in a city of ten thousand inhabitants of a hundred individuals resolved on putting an end to the violence. A city of a million will then house a thousand forest rebels—if we are to use this name before gaining an idea of its full import. This is a mighty force, sufficient to topple even powerful oppressors. For dictatorships are not only dangerous, they are at the same time endangered, since the brutal deployment of force also arouses broad resentment. Under these circumstances the resolution of even a small minority becomes cause for concern, especially if it develops a line of attack.

This explains the tremendous growth of police forces. At a first glance, the expansion of police forces into regular armies in lands with overpowering popular approval quotas may seem incongruous. It can only be an indication that the power of the minority has grown in the same relation. This is the case. Resistance should be expected under all circumstances from anyone who has dared to voted no in a so-called peace ballot—particularly if the ruling power gets into difficulties. By contrast, when things do start to get shaky, the continued support of the ninety-nine others can by no means be counted on with the same certainty. In such cases the minority is like a chemical reagent of vigorous and unforeseeable potency that percolates through the state.

To investigate, observe, and control these points of precipitation, large numbers of police are required. The mistrust grows with the approval—as the fraction of good votes approaches one hundred percent, the number of suspects only grows, since it must then be assumed that the agents of resistance have switched from a statistically determinable order to the invisible one we have characterized as the forest passage. Now an eye must be kept on everyone. The reconnaissance effort drives its organs into every city block, into every dwelling. It even tries to infiltrate the family, and its supreme victories come in the self-incriminations of the great show trials: we see the individual stepping up as his own policeman and contributing to his own elimination. No longer is he indivisible, as in the liberal world; rather, he is dissected by the state into two halves—a guilty one and another that denounces itself.

What a strange sight these proud, strutting states make: armed to the teeth and possessing all possible instruments of power, they are at the same time acutely sensitive. The care and attention they have to dedicate to their police forces diminishes their external power. The police erode the allocations for the army, and not only the allocations. Were the great masses as transparent, as aligned in their atoms as the propaganda claims, then no more police would be necessary than a shepherd needs dogs for his flock of sheep. But that is not the case, for there are wolves hiding in the gray flock—that is, characters who still know what freedom is. Moreover, these wolves are not only strong in themselves; there is also the danger that one fine morning they will transmit their characteristics to the masses, so that the flock turns into a pack. This is a ruler's nightmare.

10

A peculiar characteristic of our times is the combination of significant scenes with insignificant actors. This becomes apparent above all in our important men; the impression is of figures that one might encounter in any number in a Genevan or Viennese café, in a provincial officers' mess, or some obscure caravansary. Where intellectual traits show up that go beyond pure willpower, we can assume the survival of some older substance, as for instance in Clemenceau who may be characterized as dyed-in-the-wool.

The bothersome aspect of this spectacle is the association of such trivial stature with such enormous functional power. These are the men who make the masses tremble, whose decisions determine the fate of millions. Yet one must concede the zeitgeist an infallible hand in picking out just these characters—if we consider it in just one of its possible aspects, that of a mighty demolition enterprise. All the expropriations, devaluations, equalizations, liquidations, rationalizations, socializations, electrifications, land reallocations, redistributions, and pulverizations presuppose neither character nor cultivation, which would both actually impede the automatism. Consequently, where positions of power open up in our industrial landscapes, we observe those individuals winning the contracts whose personal insignificance is inflated by a strong will. Later we will pick up this theme again, particularly in its moral connections.

However, as the action begins to degenerate psychologically, so it becomes typologically more meaningful. Man enters into new relations, which he does not at first grasp with his consciousness, let alone through their configuration—an eye for the meaning of the scene comes only with time. And only then does sovereignty become possible: a process must first be comprehended before it can be acted upon.

With the catastrophes we see figures emerging, which prove themselves equal to the cataclysms and which will outlive them when the incidental names have been long forgotten. Among these figures is, first and foremost, that of the Worker, marching confidently and unswervingly toward its goals. The fires of downfall only serve to throw it into an ever brighter light. For the moment it still radiates an ambiguous titanic glow; we cannot yet guess the royal capitals, the cosmic metropolises in which it will erect its thrones. The world wears its uniform and its armor, and at some point it will also don its festival attire. Since it is only at the start of its career, comparisons with any previously accomplished states would be improper.

In its train other figures surface, including those in which the suffering is sublimated. One of these is the Unknown Soldier, the Nameless, who for just this reason lives not only in every capital but also in every village, in every family. The battlefields, the temporal goals, and even the peoples he has represented sink into the realm of the uncertain. As the conflagrations cool, something else remains, a shared something, and now it is no longer will and passion but art and worship that turn to it.

Why is it that this second figure is so clearly connected in our memory with the First but not the Second World War? This comes from the clear delineations that emerged from that point forward of the forms and goals of the global civil war. The soldierly aspect fell therewith into second rank. Yet the Unknown Soldier remains a hero, a conqueror of fiery worlds, who shoulders great burdens in the midst of the mechanical devastation. In this sense he is also a true descendant of western chivalry.

The Second World War is distinguished from the First not only because the national questions mix openly with and subordinate themselves to those of civil war, but also due to the escalated mechanical development, which approaches extreme limits of automatism. This brings with it intensified assaults on *nomos* and *ethos*. In this connection, utterly hopeless encirclements result from overwhelming superior forces. The material battle escalates into one of encirclement and annihilation, into a Cannae without the ancient grandeur. The suffering increases in a manner that must necessarily exclude any heroic element.

Like all strategic figures, this one too provides an exact picture of the times, which seek to resolve their issues with fire. The hopeless encirclement of man has been long in the preparation, through theories that strive for a logical and seamless explanation of the world and go hand in hand with technical development. At first there is the rational encirclement of the opponent, then the societal one; finally, at the appointed hour, he is exterminated. No more desperate fate exists than getting mixed up in a process where the law has been turned into a weapon.

11

Such phenomena have always been part of human history, and one could reckon them among the atrocities that are seldom absent wherever great changes are taking place. What is more unsettling in the present case is that the brutality is threatening to become an element, a constitutive part of the new power structures, and that we see the individual placed helplessly at their mercy.

There are a number of reasons for this, above all that rational thought is by its nature cruel. This finds its way into the planning. The elimination of free competition plays a special role in this process, and it brings forth a peculiar mirror image. As the name says, competition resembles a race, in which the most able wins the prize. Where the competitive element lapses, the threat arises of a sort of retirement at state expense, even as the external competition, the race between states, remains. It is terror that fills the resulting gap. To be sure, other circumstances precipitate the terror, and one of the reasons it endures reveals itself here: the high speed, initially induced by the competition, must now be maintained by fear. Initially, the standard depended on a high pressure, now it depends on a vacuum. Initially, the winning party set the pace, now the person who is even worse off.

In this connection, the state sees itself forced in the second case to permanently subjugate a part of the population to gruesome assaults. Life may have become gray, but it may still appear tolerable to those who see only darkness, utter blackness beside them. Here—and not in the economic realm—lie the dangers of the grand designs.

The choice of class to be persecuted is arbitrary; it will, in any case, be minorities that are either naturally distinct or artificial constructions. All those set apart by either their heritage or their talents will obviously be endangered. This climate carries over into the treatment of the defeated in wartime; accusations of collective guilt are followed by starvation in prison camps, forced labor, extermination in broad regions, and forced expulsion of any survivors.

It is understandable that people in such predicaments would rather take on the most grievous burdens than be counted among the "others." The automatism seems to effortlessly break down any remnants of free will, and the persecution concentrates and becomes as ubiquitous as an element. For a privileged few flight may remain an option, though it usually leads to something worse. Resistance only seems to invigorate the ruling powers, providing them a welcome opportunity to take offensive action. In the face of all this, the only remaining hope is that the process will be self-consuming, as a volcano exhausts itself in erupting. In the meantime, for the besieged, there can only be two concerns at this point in the game: meeting obligations and not deviating from the norm. The effects carry over into the sphere of security, where people are stricken by an apocalyptic panic.

It is at this point that the question arises, not merely theoretically but in every human existence today, whether another path remains viable. After all, there are mountain passes and mule tracks that one discovers only after a long ascent. A new conception of power has emerged, a potent and direct concentration. Holding out against this force requires a new conception of freedom, one that can have nothing to do with the washed-out ideas associated with this word today. It presumes, for a start, that one does not want to merely save one's own skin, but is also willing to risk it.

Indeed, we see that even in these states with their overpowering police forces not all movement has died out. The armor of the new Leviathans has its own weak points, which must continually be felt out, and this assumes both caution and daring of a previously unknown quality. We may imagine an elite opening this battle for a new freedom, a battle that will demand great sacrifices and which should leave no room for any interpretations that are unworthy of it. To find good comparisons we need to look back to the gravest of times and places—for instance to the Huguenots, or to the Guerrillas as Goya pictured them in his *Desastres*. By contrast, the storm of the Bastille, which still nourishes the awareness of individual freedom today, was a Sunday walk in the park.

Fundamentally, freedom and tyranny cannot be considered in isolation, although we observe them succeeding each other in time. It can clearly be said that tyranny suppresses and eliminates freedom—but, on the other hand, tyranny is only possible where freedom has been domesticated and has evaporated into vacuous concepts.

In general, man will tend to rely on the system or yield to it even when he should already be drawing on his own resources. This shows a lack of fantasy. He should know at what points he must not be induced to give up his sovereign power of decision. As long as things are in order, there will be water in the pipes and electricity in the lines. When life and property are threatened, an alarm call will summon the fire department and police. But the great danger is that man relies too heavily on this assistance and becomes helpless when it fails to materialize. Every comfort must be paid for. The condition of the domesticated animal drags behind it that of the slaughterhouse animal.

Catastrophes test the degree to which men and peoples are still natively grounded. At least one root thread must still connect directly with the earth—our health and our prospects for a life beyond civilization and its insurances depend on this connection.

This becomes evident in phases of extreme threat, during which the apparatus not only leaves man high and dry but encircles him in a manner that appears to dash all hopes of escape. At this point the individual must decide whether to give up the game or persevere from his own innermost forces. In the latter case he opts for a forest passage.

12

We previously referred to the Worker and the Unknown Soldier as two of the significant figures of our times. In the forest rebel we conceive a third figure, one that is emerging ever more clearly.

In the Worker the active principle is deployed in an attempt to pervade and master the universe in a new manner, to reach places, near and far, which no eye has ever seen, to command forces that none have ever before unleashed. In the shadow of these actions stands the Unknown Soldier, as sacrificial victim, who shoulders the burden across vast wastelands of fire, and who, as good and unifying spirit, is invoked not only within a people but also between peoples. He is the immediate son of the earth.

But, in our terms, the forest rebel is that individual who, isolated and uprooted from his homeland by the great process, sees himself finally delivered up for destruction. This could be the fate of many, indeed of all—another factor must therefore be added to the definition: this is the forest rebel's determination to resist, and his intention to fight the battle, however hopeless. The forest rebel thus possesses a primal relationship to freedom, which, in the perspective of our times, is expressed in his intention to oppose the automatism and *not* to draw its ethical conclusion, which is fatalism.

Considered in this manner, it becomes clear what role the forest passage plays, not merely in the thoughts but also in the reality of these years. Everyone finds themselves trapped in a predicament today, and the attempts we see to hold this coercion at bay resemble bold experiments upon which a far more significant destiny depends than that of those who have resolved to risk the experiment.

A gamble of this kind can only hope to succeed if the three great powers of art, philosophy, and theology come to its aid and break fresh ground in the dead-end situation. We will explore each of these themes individually. For the moment we will only say that in art the theme of the beleaguered individual is indeed gaining ground. This naturally emerges in particular in character portrayals, and in their adaptations to the stage and cinema but above all to the novel. Indeed, the perspectives are visibly changing as depictions of an advancing or disintegrating society are replaced by the individual's conflict with the technical collective and its world. In penetrating the depths of this world, the author himself becomes a forest rebel—because authorship is really only another name for independence.

A direct thread leads from these descriptions to Edgar Allan Poe. The extraordinary element in this mind is its thrift. We hear the leitmotif even before the curtain lifts, and with the first bars we realize that the scene will become sinister. The concise mathematical figures are at once also figures of destiny; that is the source of their tremendous fascination. In the maelstrom we have the funnel, the irresistible suck of emptiness, of the void. The pit provides a picture of the cauldron, of the relentlessly tightening encirclement, which constricts space and drives us onto the rats. And the pendulum is a symbol of dead, measurable time. At its end is Chronos's sharpened sickle, which swings back and forth and threatens the enchained captive, but which can also free him if he knows how to make use of it for himself.

Since then the bare grid has been filled out with oceans and continents. Historical experience has also been added. The increasingly artificial cities, the automatized traits, the wars and civil wars, the machine infernos, the gray despots, the prisons and the refined persecutions—all these have since been given names, and they occupy man's thoughts day and night. We see him as bold planner and thinker, brooding over progress but also its exit strategies; we see him in action as a machine operator, combatant, prisoner, or partisan in the heart of his cities, which at one moment are in flames, at the next bright with carnival lights. We see him as a scoffer of values and as a cold calculator—but then in despair when, from the depths of the labyrinth, his gaze searches for the stars.

The process has two poles—on one side there is the whole, striding in progressively more powerful formations through all resistance. This is the pole of consummated actions, of imperial expansion and perfect security. At the other pole there is the individual, suffering and defenseless, and in an equally perfect state of insecurity. Each pole conditions the other, since the vast unfolding of power subsists on fear, and the coercion is most effective where the sensitivity has become acute.

The countless attempts of art to assume and tackle this new situation of man as its bona fide theme go beyond mere descriptions. Rather, they are experiments with the supreme goal of uniting freedom and the world in a new harmony. Where this succeeds in an artwork, the pent-up fear must dissipate like fog with the first rays of the morning sun.

13

Fear is symptomatic of our times—and it is all the more disturbing as it comes on the heels of an epoch of great individual freedom, in which hardships of the kind portrayed by Dickens were already virtually forgotten.

How did such a shift come about? If we want to pick out a turning point none could be more appropriate than the day the Titanic went down. Here light and shadow collide starkly: the hubris of progress with panic, the highest comfort with destruction, and automatism with a catastrophe manifested as a traffic accident.

In fact, the growing automatism is closely connected with the fear, in the sense that man restricts his own power of decision in favor of technological expediencies. This brings all manner of conveniences—but an increasing loss of freedom must necessarily also result. The individual no longer stands in society like a tree in the forest; instead, he resembles a passenger on a fast-moving vessel, which could be called Titanic, or also Leviathan. While the weather holds and the outlook remains pleasant, he will hardly perceive the state of reduced freedom that he has fallen into. On the contrary, an optimism arises, a sense of power produced by the high speed. All this will change when fire-spitting islands and icebergs loom on the horizon. Then, not only does technology step over from the field of comfort into very different domains, but the lack of freedom simultaneously becomes apparent— be it in a triumph of elemental powers, or in the fact that any individuals who have remained strong command an absolute authority.

The details are well known and well described; they belong to our own-most[1] experiences. It may be objected here that other times of fear, of apocalyptic panic, have existed that were not accompanied and orchestrated by this automatic character. We leave the question open here, since the automatism only takes on a frightening aspect when it reveals itself as one of the forms, as the style, of the cataclysm—as Hieronymus Bosch so unsurpassably depicted it. Whether our modern instance represents a very unusual kind of fear or whether it is simply the return of one and the same cosmic anxiety in the style of the times—we will not pause on this but will rather raise the opposite question, which we think of crucial importance: Might it be possible to lessen the fear even as the automatism progresses or, as can be foreseen, approaches perfection? Would it not be possible to both remain on the ship *and* retain one's autonomy of decision—that is, not only to preserve but even to strengthen the roots that are still fixed in the primal ground? This is the real question of our existence.

It is this same question that is concealed behind all the fears of our times: man wants to know how he can escape

---

1. Almost certainly intended in the Heideggerian sense. *Tr.*

destruction. These days, when we sit down with acquaintances or strangers anywhere in Europe, the conversation soon turns to general concerns—and then the whole misery emerges. It becomes apparent that practically all of these men and women are in the grip of the kind of panic that has been unknown here since the early Middle Ages. We observe them plunging obsessively into their fears, whose symptoms are revealed openly and without embarrassment. We are witness to a contest of minds arguing about whether it would be better to flee, hide, or commit suicide, and who, in the possession of full liberty, are already considering the means and wiles they will employ to win the favor of the base when it comes to power. With horror we also sense that there is no infamy they will not consent to if it is demanded of them. Among them will be healthy, strapping men, built like athletes. The question must be asked: why do they bother with sports?

However, these same men are not just fearful—they are also fearsome. The sentiment changes from fear to open hate the moment they notice a weakening in those they feared only a moment before. It is not only in Europe that one comes across such congregations. Where the automatism increases to the point of approaching perfection—such as in America—the panic is even further intensified. There it finds its best feeding grounds; and it is propagated through networks that operate at the speed of light.[2] The need to hear the news several times a day is already a sign of fear; the imagination grows and paralyzes itself in a rising vortex. The myriad antennae rising above our megacities resemble hairs standing on end—they provoke demonic contacts.

2. A remarkable foreshadowing from the 1950s of the viral, almost instantaneous dissemination of news (and fear) around the planet via the internet today. Something similar may be said for the foreshadowing of twentieth-century terrorism in the paragraph that follows this one. *Tr.*

Of course, the East is not an exception in this. The West is afraid of the East, the East afraid of the West. Everywhere on the planet people live in daily expectation of terrifying attacks, and in many places there is also the fear of civil war.

The crude political mechanism is not the only cause of this fear. There are countless other anxieties; they bring with them an uncertainty that constantly sets its hopes on doctors, saviors, and miracle workers. Everything can become an object of fear. The emergence of this condition is a clearer omen of downfall than any physical danger.

14

The basic question in this vortex is whether man can be liberated from fear. This is far more important than arming or supplying him with medicines—for power and health are prerogatives of the unafraid. In contrast, the fear besets even those armed to the teeth—indeed, them above all. The same may be said for those on whom abundance has been rained. The threat cannot be exorcized by weapons or fortunes—these are no more than means.

Fear and danger are so closely correlated that it is hardly possible to say which of the two powers generates the other. Since fear is the more important, we must begin there if we are to loosen the knot.

Here we should also caution against the opposite idea—that is, of starting with the danger. Aiming simply to become more dangerous than one's feared opponent leads to no solution—this is the classic relationship between reds and whites, reds and reds, and tomorrow perhaps between whites and non-whites. Terror is a fire that wants to consume the whole world. All the while the fears multiply and diversify. The ruler by calling proves himself such by ending the terror. It is the person who has first conquered his own fear.

Moreover, it is important to know that fear will not permit itself to be banished absolutely. This also would not lead out of the automatism; on the contrary, it would convey the fear into man's inner being. When a man turns for counsel to his own heart, fear is always his principal partner in the dialogue. It will attempt to make the conversation a monologue, for only in this way can it have the last word.

If, on the other hand, the fear can be forced back into a dialogue, then man can also have his say. The illusion of encirclement will also disappear therewith, and another solution will always become visible beyond the automatic one. Two paths will then be possible—or, in other words, free choice will have been restored.

Even assuming the worst possible scenario of total ruin, a difference would remain like that between night and day. The one path climbs to higher realms, to self-sacrifice, or to the fate of those who fall with weapon in hand; the other sinks into the abysses of slave pens and slaughterhouses, where primitive beings are wed in a murderous union with technology. There are no longer destinies there—there are only numbers. To have a destiny, or to be classified as a number—this decision is forced upon all of us today, and each of us must face it *alone*. The individual today is as sovereign as an individual in any other period of history, perhaps even stronger, because as collective powers gain ground, so the individual is separated from the old established associations and must stand for himself alone. He becomes Leviathan's antagonist, indeed his conqueror and his tamer.

Let us return to the image of the election. The electoral mechanism, as we saw, has been transformed into an automatized concert under the direction of its organizer. The individual can—and will—be compelled to take part. He must only remember that all the possible positions he can assume on this field are equally null and void. Once cornered, it makes no difference whether the game runs to this or that spot in the net.

The locus of freedom is to be found elsewhere than in mere opposition, also nowhere that any flight can lead to. We have called it the forest. There, other instruments exist than a nay scribbled in its prescribed circle. Of course, we have also seen that in the state to which things have now advanced perhaps only one in a hundred is capable of a forest passage. But numerical ratios are irrelevant here—in a theater blaze it takes one clear head, a single brave heart, to check the panic of a thousand others who succumb to an animalistic fear and threaten to crush each other.

In speaking of the individual here, we mean the human being, but without the overtones that have accrued to the word over the past two centuries. We mean the free human being, as God created him. This person is not an exception, he represents no elite. Far more, he is concealed in each of us, and differences only arise from the varying degrees that individuals are able to effectuate the freedom that has been bestowed on them. In this he needs help—the help of thinkers, knowers, friends, lovers.

We might also say that man *sleeps* in the forest—and the moment he awakens to recognize his own power, order is restored. The higher rhythm present in history as a whole may even be interpreted as man's periodic rediscovery of himself. In all epochs there will be powers that seek to force a mask on him, at times totemic powers, at times magical or technical ones. Rigidity then increases, and with it fear. The arts petrify, dogma becomes absolute. Yet, since time immemorial, the spectacle also repeats of man removing the mask, and the happiness that follows is a reflection of the light of freedom.

Under the spell of powerful optical illusions we have become accustomed to viewing man as a grain of sand next to his machines and apparatuses. But the apparatuses are, and will always be, no more than a stage set for a low-grade imagination. As man has constructed them, so he can break them down or integrate them into new orders of meaning. The chains of technology can be broken—and it is the individual that has this power.

15

A potential error remains to be indicated here—that of a reliance on pure imagination. Although we will not deny that it is imagination which leads the spirit to victory, the issue cannot be reduced to the founding of yoga schools. This is the vision not only of countless sects but also of a form of Christian nihilism that oversimplifies the matter for its own convenience. For we cannot limit ourselves to knowing what is good and true on the top floors while fellow human beings are being flayed alive in the cellar. This would also be unacceptable if our position were not merely spiritually secure but also spiritually superior—because the unheard suffering of the enslaved millions cries out to the heavens. The vapors of the flayers' huts still hang in the air today; on such things there must be no deceiving ourselves.

Thus, it is not given to us to loiter in the imagination, even if imagination provides the basic force for the action. Any power struggle is preceded by a verification of images and an iconoclasm. This is why we need poets—they initiate the overthrow, even that of titans. Imagination, and with it song, belong to the forest passage.

To come back to the second of the images we are employing: The historical world in which we find ourselves resembles a fast-moving vehicle, which at one moment presents its comfort aspects, at the next its horror aspects. It is the Titanic, and it is Leviathan. Since a moving object attracts the eye, it will remain concealed to most of the ship's guests that they *simultaneously* exist in another realm, a realm of perfect stillness. This second realm is so superior as to contain the first within it like a plaything, as merely one of innumerable other manifestations. This second realm is the harbor, our homeland, the peace and security that everyone carries within them. We call it the forest.

Sea voyage and forest—uniting such disparate elements in an image may seem difficult. But myth is well-acquainted with such opposites—Dionysus, abducted by Tyrrhenian pirates, made grapevines and ivy entangle the ship's rudder and grow up over the mast. Then a tiger leaped from the thicket to tear apart the hijackers.

Myth is not prehistory; it is timeless reality, which repeats itself in history. We may consider our own century's rediscovery of meaning in myth as a favorable sign. Today, too, man has been conducted by powerful forces far out onto the ocean, deep into the deserts with their mask worlds. The journey will lose its threatening aspect the moment man recollects his own divine power.

16

There are two facts we need to know and accept if we are to escape the pattern of moves that is forced on us and play our own higher game. First, we need to understand—as in the example of the elections—that only a small fraction of the great masses will be able to defy the mighty fictions of the times and the intimidation that emanates from them. Of course, this fraction can operate in a representative role. Second, as we saw in the example of the ship, the powers of the present will be insufficient to set up a resistance.

These two statements contain nothing new. They are in the nature of things and will always impose themselves anew when catastrophes announce themselves. In such situations, the initiative will always pass into the hands of a select minority who prefer danger to servitude. And their action will always be preceded by reflection. This reflection is expressed, first, as a critique of the current epoch—that is, as a recognition of the inadequacy of the current values—and later, as retrospection. If the retrospection is directed at the fathers and their systems, which lie closer to the origins, it will seek a conservative restoration. But in times of still greater danger the salvific power must be sought deeper, in the mothers. This contact liberates primal forces, to which the mere powers of time cannot stand up.

Two characteristics are thus essential for the forest rebel: he allows no superior power to dictate the law to him, neither through propaganda nor force; and he means to defend himself, not only by exploiting the instruments and ideas of the times, but also by maintaining access to those time-transcending powers that can never be reduced to pure movement. Then he can risk the passage.

A question arises here about the purpose of such an undertaking. As we previously suggested, it cannot be limited to the conquest of purely interior realms. This is one of the notions that becomes popular in the wake of defeat. Equally unsatisfactory would be a limitation to purely concrete goals, such as conducting a national liberation struggle. Rather, as we shall see, these efforts are *also* crowned by national freedom, which joins as an additional factor. After all, we are involved not simply in a national collapse but in a global catastrophe, in which the real winners and losers can hardly be known, let alone prophesied.

It is rather the case that the ordinary man on the street, whom we meet everywhere, everyday, grasps the situation better than any regime and any theoretician. This ability stems from the surviving traces in him of a knowledge reaching deeper than all the platitudes of the times. It also explains why resolutions can be made at conferences and congresses that are much stupider and more dangerous than the candid opinion of the first random person stepping out of the next streetcar.

The individual still possesses organs in which more wisdom lives than in the entire organization—his very bewilderment, his fear, demonstrate this. In agonizing about finding a way out, an escape route, he exhibits a behavior appropriate to the proximity and magnitude of the threat. If he is skeptical about the currency and wants to get to the bottom of things, then he is simply conducting himself as someone who still knows the difference between gold and printer's ink. And if he awakens at night in terror—in a rich and peaceful country at that—this is as natural a reaction as someone's head reeling at the brink of an abyss. There is no point in trying to convince him that the abyss is not there at all. Indeed, the edge of the abyss is a good place to seek our own counsel.

How does man behave in the face of and within the catastrophe? This theme presents itself more urgently with each passing day. All the questions can be resolved into this single, most fundamental one. Even within groups of people that seem to be reciprocally conspiring against each other, the considerations basically revolve around this one same threat.

Whatever the case, it is useful to keep the catastrophe in view, as well as the ways in which one may get entangled in it. It is a good intellectual exercise. If we tackle it in the right manner, the fear will diminish, and this represents the first meaningful step toward security. The effect is not just personally beneficial; it is also preventive, since the probability of catastrophe diminishes in step with the individual's victory over fear.

17

The ship signifies being in time, the forest supra-tempo-ral being. In our nihilistic period, an optical illusion grows whereby the moving appears to increase at the expense of the resting. In truth, all the technical power that we see presently unfolding is but a fleeting shimmer from the treasure chests of being. If a man succeeds in accessing them, even for one immeasurable instant, he will gain new security—the things of time will not only lose their threatening aspect but appear newly meaningful.

Let us call this turn the Forest Passage, and the person who accomplishes it the Forest Rebel. Like Worker, this word also encompasses a spectrum of meaning, since it can designate not only very divergent forms and fields but also different lev-els of a single deportment. Although we will further refine the expression here, it is helpful that it already has a history in old Icelandic vocabulary. A forest passage followed a banishment; through this action a man declared his will to self-affirmation from his own resources. This was considered honorable, and it still is today, despite all the platitudes.

In those times, the banishment was usually the conse-quence of a homicide, whereas today it happens to a man automatically, like the turning of a roulette wheel. None of us can know today if tomorrow morning we will not be counted as part of a group considered outside the law. In that moment the civilized veneer of life changes, as the stage props of well-being disappear and are transformed into omens of destruction. The luxury liner becomes a battleship, or the black jolly roger and the red executioner's flag are hoisted on it.[3]

3. Black and red flags: likely an illusion to the NSDAP, since including these colors seems otherwise superfluous to the meaning of the sentence. The described transformation would also correspond to pre–World War II Germany: to the choice of the groups for persecution (Jews, gypsies,

In our ancestors' times, anyone banished was already accustomed to thinking for themselves, accustomed to a hard life, and to acting autonomously. Even in later times this person probably still felt strong enough within to take the banishment in stride and assume for himself not only the roles of warrior, physician, and judge, but also priest. Things are different today. People are incorporated into the collective structures in a manner that makes them very defenseless indeed. They hardly realize how irresistibly powerful the prejudices have become in our enlightened epoch. Additionally there is our whole living off of processed foods, communication connections, and utility hookups; and all the synchronizations, repetitions, and transmissions. Things are little better in the field of health. Suddenly, in the midst of such conditions, comes banishment, often like a bolt from the blue: You are red, white, black, a Russian, a Jew, a German, a Korean, a Jesuit, a Freemason—in any case, much lower than a dog. We have even on occasion observed victims joining the chorus of those condemning them.

It may be useful to those thus threatened, usually without their own recognition of their predicament, to outline their position. A strategy for their situation may emerge in this manner. In the example of the elections, we saw how cleverly disguised the traps are. First, however, let us eliminate certain remaining misconceptions attached to the expression "forest passage," which could limit its agenda by favoring a narrower set of goals.

In the first place, the forest passage should not be understood as a form of anarchism directed against the machine world, although the temptation is strong, particularly when the effort simultaneously aims at reconnecting with myth. The

communists, etc.), to the new well-being that ultimately heralded war and catastrophe. *Tr.*

mythical will undoubtedly come; it is already on its way. In reality, the mythical is always present, and at the given moment it rises like a treasure to the surface. But it will emerge from the movement, as a heterogeneous principle, only at its highest, supremely developed stage. In this sense the movement is only the mechanism, the cry of birth. There is no return to the mythical; rather, it is encountered again when time is shaken to its foundations, and in the presence of extreme danger. Neither is it a question of the grapevine or—it is rather the grapevine *and* the ship. The numbers of those wanting to abandon ship is growing, among them sharp minds and sound spirits. This would amount to jumping off in mid-ocean. Then hunger, cannibalism, and the sharks arrive—in short, all the terrors of the raft of the Medusa. It is thus under all circumstances advisable to stay on board and on deck, even at the risk of being blown up with everything else.

This objection is not directed at the poet, who, in his works and in his life, manifests the vast superiority of the world of the muses over the technical world. He helps people find the way back to themselves—the poet is a forest rebel.

No less dangerous would be to limit the word to the German struggle for freedom. The catastrophe has precipitated Germany into a position that makes a military reorganization indispensable. Such a reform has not happened since the defeat of 1806: the armies, although dramatically changed, in scale as well as in tactics and technology, are still premised, like all our political establishments, on the basic ideas of the French Revolution. A true reorganization of the military would also not consist in adapting the army to aerial or nuclear strategies. Instead, it regards a new idea of freedom gaining force and form, as happened in the revolutionary armies after 1789 and in the Prussian army after 1806. In this respect, other deployments of military power than those drawing force from the principles of total mobilization undoubtedly remain possible today. These principles, however, are not subordinated to the interests of nations but are adoptable wherever freedom reawakens in man. From a technical perspective we have reached a state where only two powers are still fully autarkic—that is, in a position to sustain a political strategy involving an arsenal of weapons sufficiently large for objectives on a planetary scale. A forest passage, on the other hand, is possible everywhere on the planet.

With this we also want to make clear that there are no veiled anti-eastern designs in this expression. The fear that circulates on our planet today is largely inspired by the east, and it is expressed in tremendous preparations, in material and intellectual spheres. As obvious as this may appear, it is not a basic motive but rather a consequence of the international situation. The Russians are in the same straits as everyone else; indeed, if fear is the measure, they are possibly still more strongly in its grip. But fear cannot be diminished by armaments, only by gaining a new access to freedom. In this respect, Russians and Germans still have plenty to share with each other, for they share the same experiences. For Russians, too, the forest passage is the central issue. As a Bolshevik, he finds himself on the ship; as a Russian, he is in the forest. This relation both endangers him and assures his security.

However, our intention is not at all to occupy ourselves with the foreground technicalities of the politics and its groupings. They sweep by while the threat remains, indeed returns more quickly and aggressively with every moment. The opponents come so to resemble each other that they are easily recognized as masks of one and the same power. It is not a question of prevailing over the phenomenon here or there, but rather of getting time itself under control. This requires sovereignty—and this will be found less in the great resolutions than in the individual who has renounced his inner fear. In the end, all the enormous preparations, which are directed solely at him, can only bring his triumph. This knowledge liberates him. The dictatorships then sink into the dust. These are the scarcely explored reserves of our times, and not only of ours. This freedom constitutes the theme of history in general, and it marks off its boundaries: on one side against the demonic realms, on the other against the merely zoological event. This is prefigured in myth and in religions, and it always returns; so, too, the giants and the titans always manifest with the same apparent superiority. The free man brings them down; and he need not always be a prince or a Hercules. A stone from a shepherd's sling, a flag raised by a virgin, and a crossbow have already proven sufficient.

18

Another question arises in this connection. To what extent is freedom desirable, even meaningful, in the context of our particular historical situation? Does an exceptional and easily undervalued merit of contemporary man not perhaps lie precisely in his capacity to surrender large portions of his freedom? In many respects he resembles a soldier on the march to unknown destinations, or a worker constructing a palace that others will inhabit—and this is certainly not among his worst traits. Should he then be redirected while the movement is still in progress?

Anyone seeking to extract elements of meaning from events bound up with so much suffering only makes himself a stumbling block for others. That said, all prognoses that are based simply on a doom and gloom scenario miss the point. It is rather the case that we find ourselves traversing a series of increasingly defined images, increasingly distinct impressions. Catastrophes barely interrupt the development, indeed they abbreviate it in many aspects. There can be no doubt that the whole thing has its objectives. Millions live under the spell of this prospect, lead lives that would be intolerable without it and inexplicable by pure coercion alone. The sacrifices may be compensated late, but they will not have been in vain.

We touch here on the element of necessity, of destiny, which determines the gestalt of the Worker. There can be no birth without pain. The processes will continue, and, as in all fateful situations, attempts to arrest and return them to their points of departure can only foster and accelerate them.

To avoid losing the way among mirages, it is therefore a good idea to always keep the necessary in mind. Yet the necessary is given us *with* its freedom, and a new order can only constitute itself once these two establish a new relation with each other. In a temporal perspective, all changes in the necessary bring with them changes in freedom. This is why the concepts of freedom of 1789 have become untenable and ineffective in controlling the violence. Freedom *itself*, on the other hand, is immortal, though always dressed in the garments of the times. Moreover, it must be earned each time anew. Inherited freedom must be reasserted in the forms that the encounter with historical necessity impresses on it.

Admittedly, asserting one's freedom today has become especially difficult. Resistance demands great sacrifice, which explains why the majority prefer to accept the coercion. Yet genuine history can only be made by the free; history is the stamp that the free person gives to destiny. In this sense, he can naturally act in a representative manner; his sacrifice will count for the others too.

Let us assume that we have investigated the contours of the hemisphere in which the necessary is consummated. On this end, the technical, the typical, and the collective aspects stand out, at times grandiose, at others terrifying. Now we approach the other pole, where the individual presents himself, not only as sufferer but also as knower and judge. Here the contours change; they become freer and more spiritual, but the dangers also become more apparent.

Nevertheless, it would have been impossible to start with this part of the task, since the necessary is given first. It may come our way as coercion, as sickness, as chaos, even as death—in any event, it must be understood as a test.

Things cannot, therefore, come down to a question of modifying the blueprint of the work world; if anything, the great destruction lays the plans bare. That said, other edifices could certainly be erected than the termite mounds that the utopias partly foster, partly dread; the project is not as simplistic as all that. Neither is it a question of refusing to pay the times the toll they demand: duty and freedom can be reconciled.

<h2 style="text-align:center">19</h2>

Here is another objection to consider: Should we count on catastrophe? Should we—if only intellectually—seek out the most distant waters, the cataracts, the maelstroms, the great abysses?

The objection should not be underestimated. There is much to be said for staking out the safe routes that reason suggests, and sticking to them with all our will. This dilemma also has practical aspects, for example concerning armaments. Armaments exist for the eventuality of war, in the first place as a means of security. But then they lead to a threshold beyond which they themselves push on toward war, even appear to attract it. A level of investment occurs here that can only lead to bankruptcy. Picture a system of lightning conductors that eventually even brings on the thunderstorms.

The same holds true in the intellectual domain. By fixating our imagination on the most extreme routes, we overlook the road in front of us. However, here too, the one need not exclude the other. Rather, reason demands that we ponder the possibilities in their totality and prepare a response for *each* of them, like a series of chess moves.

In our present situation we are obliged to reckon with catastrophe, even take the possibility to bed with us, so that it does not surprise us in the middle of the night. Only in this manner can we accumulate a reserve of security that will make well-reasoned action possible. In a state of perfect security, the mind only plays with the idea of catastrophe; it integrates it as an unlikely power in its plans and covers the risk with a modest insurance. In our times things are the opposite. We must direct practically all our capital to the catastrophe—in order to merely keep a middle way open, a way that has in any case become as narrow as a razor's edge.

Knowledge of the middle way put forward by reason is indispensable; it is like a compass needle that reveals every movement, including any deviation. Only thus can we arrive at norms that all will recognize, without coercion. In this manner the legal boundaries will also be respected; in the long run, this way leads to victory.

That a legal path can exist which all basically recognize—of this there can be no doubt. We are plainly moving away from the national states, away from the large partitions, toward planetary orders. These can be achieved by covenants and conventions, assuming only the good will of the partners. Above all, this would have to be demonstrated by an easing of sovereignty demands—for there is fertility concealed in renunciation. Ideas and also facts exist upon which a mighty peace could be established. But this presupposes that borders be respected: annexations of provinces, resettlements of populations, the creation of corridors and divisions along lines of latitude—these only perpetuate the violence. In this sense it is even advantageous that peace has not yet been achieved, and that the iniquity has not thereby gained official sanction.

The peace of Versailles already contained the seeds of the Second World War. Based as it was on open force, it provided the gospel upon which each future act of violence was based. A second peace of this nature would have an even shorter life and destroy Europe.

Let us move on, since we are interested in other than political ideas here. Our concern is far more the imperilment of the individual and his fear. He is preoccupied with the same conflict. Fundamentally, he is motivated by the desire to devote himself to family and career, to follow his natural inclinations; but then the times assert themselves—be it in a gradual deterioration of conditions, or that he suddenly senses an attack from extremist positions. Expropriations, forced labor, and worse appear in his vicinity. It quickly becomes clear to him that neutrality would be tantamount to suicide—now it is a case of joining the wolf pack or going to war against it.

Caught in such straits, where is he to find a third element that will not simply go under in the movement? This can only be in his quality of being an individual, in his human Being, which remains unshaken. In such conditions it should be considered a great merit if knowledge of the virtuous way is not entirely lost. Anyone who has escaped the clutches of catastrophe knows that he basically had the help of simple people to thank, people who were not overcome by the hate, the terror, the mechanicalness of platitudes. These people withstood the propaganda and its plainly demonic insinuations. When such virtues also manifest in a leader of people, endless blessings can result, as with Augustus for example. This is the stuff of empires. The ruler reigns not by taking but by giving life. And therein lies one of the great hopes: that one perfect human being will step forth from among the millions.

So much for the theory of catastrophes. We are not at liberty to avoid them, yet there is freedom in them. They are one of our trials.

20

The teaching of the forest is as ancient as human history, and even older. Traces can already be found in the venerable old documents that we are only now partly learning to decipher. It constitutes the great theme of fairy tales, of sagas, of the sacred texts and mysteries. If we assign the fairy tale to the stone age, myth to the bronze age, and history to the iron age, we will stumble everywhere across this teaching, assuming our eyes are open to it. We will rediscover it in our own uranian epoch, which we might also call the age of radiation.

The knowledge that primal centers of power are hidden in the mutating landscapes, founts of superabundance and cosmic power within the ephemeral phenomena, may be found always and everywhere. This knowledge comprises not only the symbolic sacramental foundation of the churches, its threads weave not only through esoteric doctrines and sects, but it also constitutes the nucleus of philosophical systems, however divergent these conceptual worlds may be. Fundamentally, all aim at this same mystery, a mystery that lies open to anyone who has once been initiated into it—be it conceived as idea, as original monad, as thing-in-itself, or, in our own day, as existence. Anyone who has once touched being has crossed the threshold where words, ideas, schools, and confessions still matter. Yet, in the process, he has also learned to revere that which is the life force of all of them.

In this sense the word "forest" is also not the point. Naturally, it is no coincidence that all our bonds to timely cares so marvelously melt away the moment our glance falls on flowers and trees and is drawn into their spell. Here would be the right line of approach for a spiritual elevation of botany. For here we find the Garden of Eden, the vineyard, the lily, the grain of wheat of Christian parable. We find the enchanted forest of fairy tales with its man-eating wolves, its witches and giants; but also the good hunter, and the sleeping beauty of the rose hedges in whose shadow time stands still. Here, too, are the forests of the Germans and Celts, like the Glasur woods in which the heroes defeat death—and, again, Gethsemane and its olive groves.

But the same thing is also sought in other places—in caves, in labyrinths, in the desert where the tempter lives. To those who can divine its symbols a tremendous life force inhabits all things and places. Moses strikes his staff on the rock and the water of life spurts forth. A moment like this then suffices for millenia.

All this only *seems* to have been given to remote places and times. In reality, it is concealed in every individual, entrusted to him in code, so that he might understand himself, in his deepest, supra-individual power. This is the goal of every teaching that is worthy of the name. Let matter condense into veritable walls that seem to block all prospects: yet the abundance is closest at hand, for it lives within man as a gift, as a time-transcending patrimony. It is up to him how he will grasp the staff: to merely support him on his life path, or to serve him as a scepter.

Time provides us with new parables. We have unlocked forms of energy vastly more powerful than any previously known; yet this remains but a parable, for the formulas that human science discovers over time always lead back to that which has already long been known. The new lights, the new suns are passing flares that detach from the spirit. They verify the absolute in man, the miraculous power that is in him. And time and again it is the same strokes of fate that return to challenge him—not as this man or that, but as man per se.

This great theme also carries through music: the changing figures lead the drama to the point where man encounters himself in his time-transcending dimensions, where he himself becomes an instrument of destiny. This is the supreme, most awesome invocation, to which only the master is entitled who knows how to guide us through the gates of judgment to salvation.

Man has immersed himself too deeply in the constructions, he has devalued himself and lost contact with the ground. This brings him close to catastrophe, to great danger, and to pain. They drive him into untried territory, lead him toward destruction. How strange that it is just there—ostracized, condemned, fleeing—that he encounters himself anew, in his undivided and indestructible substance. With this he passes through the mirror images and recognizes himself in all his might.

21

The forest is *heimlich*, secret. This is one of those words in the German language that simultaneously contains its opposite. The secret is the intimate, the well-protected home, the place of safety. But it is no less the clandestine, and in this sense it approaches the *unheimlich*, that which is uncanny or eerie. Whenever we stumble across roots like this, we may be sure that the great contradictions sound in them—and the even greater equivalences—of life and death, whose solution was the concern of the mysteries.

In this light the forest is the great house of death, the seat of annihilating danger. It is the task of the spiritual guide to lead his charge there by the hand, that he may lose his fear. He lets him die symbolically, and resurrect. A step before annihilation awaits triumph. The initiate who learns this is elevated beyond the powers of time. He learns that they can fundamentally do him no harm, indeed that they only exist to confirm his highest possibilities. The terrifying arsenal, set to devour him, is gathered around him. The picture is not new. The "new" worlds are always only copies of one and the same world. The gnostics, the desert hermits, the fathers, and the true theologians have known this world since the beginning. They knew the word that would fell the apparitions. The serpent of death was transformed into the staff, into the scepter of the initiate who seized it.

Fear always takes on the mask, the style of the times. The gloomy vault of outer space, the visions of hermits, the spawn of Bosch and Cranach, the covens of witches and demons of the Middle Ages—all are links in the eternal chain of fear that shackles man, like Prometheus to the Caucasus. From whichever heavenly pantheon man may free himself, yet fear will stick, cunningly, at his side. And it will always appear to him as supreme, paralyzing reality. A man may join the realms of rigorous knowledge and ridicule earlier spirits who were so terrified by Gothic schemas and infernal imagery. Yet he will hardly suspect that he is caught in the same chains. The phantoms that test him will naturally conform to the style of knowledge, will appear as scientific facts. The old forest may have become a managed woodland, an economic factor; yet a lost child still strays in it. Now the world is a battlefield for armies of microbes; the apocalypse threatens as it always did, only now as the doings of physics. The old delusions continue to flourish in psychoses and neuroses. Even the man-eating ogre can be recognized again through his transparent cloak—and not only as exploiter and taskmaster in the bone mills of our times. More likely he will appear as a serologist, sitting among his instruments and retorts and pondering how to use human spleen or breastbone to produce marvelous new medicines. We are back in the heart of Dahomey, in old Mexico.

This is all no less fictitious than the edifice of any other symbol world whose ruins we excavate from a pile of rubble. Like them, it too will pass away, crumble, and become incomprehensible to alien eyes. Then other fictions will rise from the inexhaustible womb of being, just as convincing, just as diverse and as flawlessly complete.

It is advantageous that in our present condition we are at least not wasting away in complete torpor. For we ascend not only to great heights of self-awareness, but also to severe self-criticism. This a sign of high cultures, which raise their vaults above the dream world. Through our particular style, that of knowledge, we achieve insights analogous to the Indian image of the veil of Maya, or to Zarathustra's teaching of the eternal recurrence of the same. Indian wisdom assigns even the rise and fall of divine realms to the world of illusion, to the foam of time. In this regard we cannot agree with Zimmer's view that a similar greatness of vision is absent in our times. It is merely that we grasp it in the style of knowledge, which passes everything through the pulverizing mill of epistemology. Here shimmer the very limits of time and space. The same process, perhaps still more condensed and farther reaching, is repeating today in the turn from knowledge to being. In addition, there is the triumph of cyclic conceptions in the philosophy of history. Of course, this must be complemented by a knowledge of *historia in nuce*: that it is always the same theme, which is modified in endless variations of time and space. In this sense there exists not only a history of cultures but also of humanity, which, in its substance, *in nuce*, is a history of man. It recurs in the course of each human life.

With this we have returned to our theme. At all times, in all places, and in every heart, human fear is the same: it is the fear of destruction, the fear of death. We can already hear it in

Gilgamesh, we hear it in Psalm 90, and to this day nothing has changed.

To overcome the fear of death is at once to overcome every other terror, for they all have meaning only in relation to this fundamental problem. The forest passage is, therefore, above all a passage through death. The path leads to the brink of death itself—indeed, if necessary, it passes through it. When the line is successfully crossed, the forest as a place of life is revealed in all its preternatural fullness. The superabundance of the world lies before us.

Every authentic spiritual guidance is related to this truth—it knows how to bring man to the point where he recognizes the reality. This is most evident where the teaching and the example are united: when the conqueror of fear enters the kingdom of death, as we see Christ, the highest benefactor, doing. With its death, the grain of wheat brought forth not a thousand fruits, but fruits without number. The superabundance of the world was touched, which every generative act is related to as a symbol of time, and of time's defeat. In its train followed not only the martyrs, who were stronger than the stoics, stronger than the caesars, stronger than the hundred thousand spectators surrounding them in the arena—there also followed the innumerable others who died with their faith intact. To this day this is a far more compelling force than it at first seems. Even when the cathedrals crumble, a patrimony of knowledge remains that undermines the palaces of the oppressors like catacombs. Already on these grounds we may be sure that the pure use of force, exercised in the old manner, cannot prevail in the long term. With this blood, substance was infused into history, and it is with good reason that we still number our years from this epochal turning point. The full fertility of theogony reigns here, the mythical generative power. The sacrifice is replayed on countless altars.

In his poems Hölderlin saw Christ as the exaltation of Herculean and Dionysian power. Hercules is the original prince, on whom even the gods depend in their battle with the titans. He dries out the swamps and builds canals, and, by defeating the fiends and monsters, he makes the wastelands habitable. He is first among the heroes, on whose graves the polis is founded, and by whose veneration it is preserved. Every nation has its Hercules, and even today graves form the central points from which the state receives its sacred luster.

Dionysus is the master of ceremonies, the leader of the festive procession. When Hölderlin refers to him as the spirit of community, this community is to be understand as including the dead, indeed especially them. Theirs is the glow that envelopes the Dionysian celebration, the deepest fount of cheerfulness. The doors of the kingdom of death are thrown wide open, and golden abundance streams forth. This is the meaning of the grapevine, in which the powers of earth and sun are united, of the masks, of the great transformation and recurrence.

Among men we remember Socrates, who provided a fruitful example not only for the Stoics but for intrepid spirits of all times. We may hold different views on the life and teachings of this man; his death, in any case, was among the greatest events. The world is so constituted that its passions and prejudices always demand a tribute in blood, and we should know that this will never be otherwise. The arguments may change, but ignorance will eternally hold court. Man is charged for being contemptuous of the gods, then for not bending to a dogma, and later again for having repudiated a theory. There exists no great word and no noble thought for which blood has not flowed. It is Socratic to understand that the judgment is invalid—to understand this in a more elevated sense than any merely human for-and-against can establish. The true judgment is spoken from the beginning; its purpose is to exalt the sacrifice. Therefore, if modern Greeks were ever to seek an appeal of this sentence, it would only be one more useless gloss on world history—particularly in a period in which the innocent blood flows in rivers. This trial is never-ending, and we met the philistines sitting as its judges on every street corner today, in every parliament. That this could only change: since the earliest times, this thought has always distinguished superficial minds. Human greatness must ever and again be won anew. Victory comes when the assault of the ignoble is beaten back in one's own breast. Here is the authentic substance of history: in man's encounter with himself, that is, with his own divine power. Anyone aspiring to teach history should know this. Socrates called this most profound place, from which a voice advised and directed him—no longer even with words— his Daimonion. We could also call it the forest.

What would it now mean for a contemporary man to take his lead from the example of death's champion, of these gods, heroes, and sages? It would mean that he join the resistance against the times, and not merely against these times, but against all times, whose basic power is fear. Every fear, however distantly derived it may seem, is at its core the fear of death. If a man succeeds in creating breathing room here, he will gain freedom also in other spheres that are ruled by fear. Then he will fell the giants whose weapons are terror. This, too, has recurred again and again in history.

It is in the nature of things that education today aims at precisely the opposite of this. Never have such strange ideas prevailed in the teaching of history as today. The intention in all systems is to inhibit any metaphysical influx, to tame and train in the interests of the collective. Even in circumstances where the Leviathan finds itself dependent on courage, on the battlefield for instance, it will seek to simulate a second, even more ominous threat to keep the fighter at his post. Such states depend on their police.

The great solitude of the individual is a hallmark of our times. He is surrounded, encircled by fear, which pushes walls in against him on all sides. This takes on concrete forms—in prisons, in slavery, in battles of encirclement. The thoughts, the soliloquies, perhaps even the diaries from the years when even the neighbors could not be trusted, are filled with this material.

Politics drives into other zones here—be it natural history, or demonic history with all its horrors. At the same time powerful forces of salvation are sensed close at hand. The terrors are wake-up calls; they are signs of quite other dangers than those projected by the historical conflicts. They amount to increasingly urgent questions posed to man. Nobody can answer for him but himself.

22

At this threshold man is initiated into his theological trial, whether he realizes it or not. Again, we should not put inordinate weight on the word. Man is interrogated about his supreme values, about his view of the world as a whole and the relationship of his existence to it. This need not happen in words, indeed it eludes the word. It is also not about the particular formulation of the answer; that is, it is not a question of this confession or that.

We can thus leave aside the churches. There are significant indications today—indeed, especially today—that attest to the unexhausted good contained in them. Above all there is the attitude of their opponents, in the first place that of the state, which aspires to absolute power. This necessarily leads to persecution of the churches. In the new state of affairs man is to be handled as a zoological being, regardless of whether the theories predominating at the time categorize him along economic or other lines. This leads at first into zones of pure utility, thereafter to bestial exploitation.

On the other hand there is the institutional character of the church, as a man-made organization. In this regard there is the constant threat of rigidification and the consequent drying up of its beneficent forces. This explains the gloomy, mechanical, and nonsensical aspects of many church services, the recurring Sunday torment, and of course sectarianism. The institutional element is at the same time the vulnerable aspect; weakened by doubt, the edifice crumbles overnight—if it has not simply been transformed into a museum. We need to reckon with times and regions where the church simply no longer exists. The state will then see itself called upon to fill the gap that has resulted, or been revealed, with its own means— an enterprise in which it can only fail.

For those who are not to be so crudely fobbed off, the prospect of a forest passage presents itself. The priestly type, someone who believes that a higher life is impossible with- out sacrament and sees his calling in satisfying this hunger, may find himself forced into such a passage. It leads into the forest, to a form of existence that always recurs after perse- cutions and that has often been described: in the story of the holy Polycarp,[4] for example; or in the memoirs of the excel- lent d'Aubigné,[5] Henry IV's Master of the Horse. In more

4. Polycarp (69–155) was a second-century Christian bishop of Smyrna. He died a martyr, burned at the stake for refusing to burn incense to the emperor. *Tr.*

5. Théodore-Agrippa d'Aubigné (1552–1630) was a French nobleman, militant Protestant, and chronicler. His epic poem *Les Tragiques* (1616) is regarded as his masterpiece. He served Henry IV of France (Henry of Navarre) in the religious wars of the time between Catholics and Protes- tants. In reaction to the king's opportunistic conversion to Catholicism, he retreated to his landed estates. *Tr.*

modern times, we could name Graham Greene and his novel *The Power and the Glory*, with its tropical setting. Naturally, the forest in this sense is everywhere; it can even be in a metropolitan neighborhood.

Beyond that it will also be a necessity for any individuals who cannot resign themselves to mere functions in the zoological-political arrangement. With this we touch on the essence of modern suffering, the great emptiness that Nietzsche characterized as the growth of the deserts. The deserts grow: this is the spectacle of civilization with its vacuous relationships. In this landscape the question of provisions becomes especially urgent, especially haunting: "The desert grows, woe to him in whom deserts hide."

It is a good thing if churches can create oases—but a better thing still if man does not content himself with that. The church can provide assistance but not existence. Here, too, from an institutional perspective, we are still on the ship, still in motion; peace lies in the forest. The decision takes place in man, and none can take it off his hands.

The desert grows: the fallow and barren circles expand. First the meaningfully arranged quarters disappear: the gardens whose fruits we innocently fed on, the rooms equipped with well-proven instruments. Then the laws become questionable, the apparatuses double-edged. Woe to him in whom deserts hide: woe to him who carries within not one cell of that primal substance that ensures fertility, again and again.

23

There are two touch- and milestones that no one today can avoid—they are doubt and pain, the two great instruments of the nihilistic reduction. One has to have passed by them. This is the challenge, the matriculation test for a new age, and none will be spared it. For this reason things have advanced incomparably further in some countries of our planet than in others, perhaps precisely in those countries we consider undeveloped. This would belong in a chapter on optical illusions.

What is the terrible question that the void poses to man? It is the ancient riddle of the Sphinx to Oedipus. Man is interrogated about himself—does he know the name of the curious being that moves through time? Depending on his answer, he will be devoured or crowned. The void wants to know if man is equal to it, whether there are elements in him that no time can destroy. In this sense, the void and time are identical; and so it is understandable that with the great power of the void time becomes very valuable, even in its tiniest fractions. At the same time, the apparatuses continue to multiply—that is, the arsenal of time. This results in the error that it is the apparatuses, in particular machine technology, that render the world void. The opposite is true: the apparatuses grow relentlessly and draw ever closer because an answer is again due to the age-old question to man. The apparatuses are witnesses that time needs to demonstrate to the senses its superiority. If man answers correctly, the apparatuses lose their magical gleam and submit themselves to his hand. It is important to realize this.

We have touched here on the fundamental issue: time's question to man about his power. It is directed at his substance. All that may emerge in the form of hostile empires, weapons, and hardships belongs only to the mise-en-scène by which the drama is staged. There can be no doubt that man will once again conquer time, will banish the void back into its hole.

A sign of this interrogation is loneliness, something remarkable in times with such a flourishing cult of community. Yet few will be spared the experience that it is precisely the collective that takes on an inhumane aspect today. And there is a second, similar paradox: that the freedom of the individual is increasingly restricted in direct correspondence to the tremendous conquest of space in general.

With this observation on loneliness we might end the chapter here—for what use can there be in bringing up situations to which neither helpful means nor spiritual guides can get through? There is a tacit agreement that this is our situation, as there are also things that we only reluctantly discuss. A positive trait of contemporary man is his reserved attitude toward lofty platitudes, his objective need for intellectual honesty. There is additionally the particular quality of his consciousness that can discern even the subtlest false note. At least in this respect people still have a sense of shame.

Nonetheless, this is a forum where significant things are taking place. Someday, perhaps, those parts of our literature that sprung from the least literary intentions may be perceived as its most powerful voices: all the narratives, letters, and diaries that came into existence in the great witch hunts, in the encirclements, and in the flaying huts of our world. It will be recognized then that man had reached a depth in his *de profundis* that touched the bedrock of being and broke the tyrannical power of doubt. In that moment, he lost his fear.

The manner in which such an attitude forms, even when it ultimately fails, can be followed in the notes of Petter Moen,[6]

6. Petter Moen, a conventional middle-class Norwegian who worked as an insurance agent, joined the Norwegian resistance when the Germans invaded his country. He became the editor of an underground newspaper in Oslo until his arrest in 1944 by the Gestapo. They detained him for 214 days, 75 of them in solitary confinement, and tortured him. Without writing materials, he used a pin to prick out words and sentences on toilet paper. Regarding his complete lack also of reading materials, he noted in this laboriously produced diary: "It's very useful to be without reference books. I must find the solution myself." Though apparently without previous interest in theology or metaphysics, he found faith "for one second or two" on his thirty-second day of confinement, but he lost it some days later when other prisoners joined him in his cell. He died in September 1944 with the sinking

discovered in the air shaft of his prison cell. Moen, a Norwegian who died in German imprisonment, can be considered a spiritual successor of Kierkegaard. In almost all cases when such letters are preserved, also those of Graf Moltke[7] for instance, a fortunate coincidence is involved. Cracks like these provide insights into a world believed to have died out. We should still see documents from Bolshevik Russia joining these, to complement and add previously unknown meaning to what we thought to have observed there.

<h2 style="text-align:center">24</h2>

Another question is this: how is man to be prepared for paths that lead into darkness and the unknown? The fulfillment of this task belongs chiefly to the churches, and in many known, and many more unknown, cases, it has effectively been accomplished. It has been confirmed that greater force can be preserved in churches and sects than in what are today called worldviews—which usually means natural science raised to the level of philosophical conviction. It is for this reason that we see tyrannical regimes so rabidly persecuting such

of the transport ship SS Westfalen. His diary was translated into English in 1951. *Tr.*

7. Helmut James Graf von Moltke was an aristocratic German jurist and devout Christian who was involved in subversive activities against German human rights abuses in German-occuppied territories. He later founded the Kreisau Circle resistance group, which acted against the government of Adolf Hitler. The Gestapo convicted von Moltke on invented evidence of conspiracy and executed him in January 1945. His Kreisau Circle discussed primarily the development of moral and democratic principles for a post-Hitler Germany, in some respects enacting the ground-preparing role for new freedoms that Jünger also describes in this work for the forest rebel. The letters Jünger refers to are presumably those secretly written to his wife Freya, also a member of the Kreisau Circle, while he was imprisoned in Berlin. English translation: Helmuth James von Moltke, *Letters to Freya: 1939–1945*, trans. Beate Ruhm von Oppen (New York: Knopf, 1990). *Tr.*

harmless creatures as the Jehovah's Witnesses—the same tyrannies that reserve seats of honor for their nuclear physicists.

It shows a healthy instinct that today's youth is beginning to show new interest in religion. Even if the churches should prove themselves unable to cater to this instinct, the initiative is important because it creates a framework for comparisons. It reveals what was possible in the past, and hence what one may be justified in expecting from the future. What was possible is still recognizable today in only a single limited field, that of art history. Yet the futurists were at least right about one thing: that all the paintings, palaces, and museum cities mean nothing in comparison with the primal creative force. The mighty current that left all these creations in its wake like colorful seashells can never run dry—it continues to flow deep underground. If man looks into himself, he will rediscover it. And with that he will create points in the desert where oases become possible.

Yet we do need to reckon with broad regions in which churches either no longer exist or have themselves withered into organs of the tyranny. Still more important is the consideration that in many people today a strong need for religious ritual coexists with an aversion to churches. There is a sense of something missing in existence, which explains all the activity around gnostics, founders of sects, and evangelists, who all, more or less successfully, step into the role of the churches. One might say that a certain definite quantity of religious faith always exists, which in previous times was legitimately satisfied by the churches. Now, freed up, it attaches itself to all and everything. This is the gullibility of modern man, which coexists with a lack of faith. He believes what he reads in the newspaper but not what is written in the stars.

The gap created here is perceptible even in fully secularized existence, and there is consequently no lack of attempts to close it with available means. A book like Bry's *Disguised Religion*[8] provides insight into this world in which science departs from its proper field and gains conventicle founding power. Often it is even the same individual in whom the science waxes and then wanes, as can be followed for instance in the careers of Haeckel or Driesch.

Since the loss makes itself felt above all as suffering, it should not be surprising that doctors in particular apply themselves to the problem, with subtle systems for sounding the depths and therapies based on these. Among the most common category of patients that they seek to help are those who want to kill their fathers. Another type—those who have lost their fathers and suffer from an unawareness of their loss—will be sought in vain among their patients. This futility is with good reason, for medicine is impotent at this point. Certainly, there must be something of a priest in every good doctor; but the thought of taking over for the priest can only occur to doctors in times when the distinction between salvation and health has been lost. Therefore, we may think what we want about the various imitations of such spiritual instruments and forms as examinations of conscience, confession, meditation, prayer, ecstasy, and others—none of the imitations reach deeper than the symptoms, if they are not actually harmful.

Attempts to refer back to higher worlds to which access has disappeared can only increase the inner erosion. A depiction of the suffering, a diagnosis, is more important—a precise circumscription of what has been lost. Curiously, this is more easily found in a convincing form in writers than in

8. Carl Christian Bry (1892–1926) was a German author known for his *Verkappte Religionen: Kritik des kollektiven Wahns* (*Disguised Religion: A Critique of Collective Insanity*, untranslated). In this work he also classified National Socialism as a religious utopia capable of inducing a "collective insanity." *Tr.*

theologians, from Kierkegaard to Bernanos. As we said earlier, a balance remains open to this day only in art history. Now it is also necessary to make a balance visible for the human power of the individual. But we should not look to the field of ethics to fulfill this task, for it really lies in that of existence. A person scraping by, if not in an actual wasteland then in a wasted zone such as an industrial city, to whom a mere glimmer, a brief whiff of the immense power of being is imparted—such a person begins to sense that something is missing in his life. This is the prerequisite for him to start searching. Now it is important that it is a theologian who removes the scales from his eyes, because only in this way will this seeker have any prospect of reaching his goal. All other faculties, not to even mention the merely practical ones, would only send him off chasing mirages. Apparently, in the great syllabus of mankind there are a certain number of such pictures that must first be successfully passed—utopic passages, transfigured by the perspective of progress. Whether progress projects before man images of universal dominion, termite-like ideal states, or realms of eternal peace—where an authentic mandate is lacking, this will all prove illusionary. In this respect, the Germans have paid enormous dues for their apprenticeship; yet, if they are able to sincerely grasp these as such, it will prove to be well-spent capital.

Theologians of today must be prepared to deal with people as they are today—above all with people who do not live in sheltered reserves or other lower pressure zones. A man stands before them who has emptied his chalice of suffering and doubt, a man formed far more by nihilism than by the church—ignoring for the moment how much nihilism is concealed in the church itself. Typically, this person will be little developed ethically or spiritually, however eloquent he may be in convincing platitudes. He will be alert, intelligent,

active, skeptical, inartistic, a natural-born debaser of higher
types and ideas, an insurance fanatic, someone set on his own
advantage, and easily manipulated by the catchphrases of
propaganda whose often abrupt turnabouts he will hardly perceive; he will gush with humanitarian theory, yet be equally
inclined to awful violence beyond all legal limits or international law whenever a neighbor or fellow human being does
not fit into his system. At the same time he will feel haunted
by malevolent forces, which penetrate even into his dreams,
have a low capacity to enjoy himself, and have forgotten the
meaning of a real festival. On the other hand, it must be added
that he enjoys the advantages of a peaceful age of technological comfort: that the average life expectancy has significantly
risen; that the basic tenets of theoretical equality are universally recognized; and that, in some places at least, there are
models to be studied of lifestyles that, in their comfort for
all levels of society, their individual freedoms, and automatized perfection, have perhaps never existed before. It is not
unthinkable that this lifestyle will spread after the titanic era of
technology has run its course. Just the same, man is suffering a
loss, and this loss explains the manifest grayness and hopeless-
ness of his existence, which in some cities and even in whole
lands so overshadows life that the last smiles have been extinguished and people seem trapped in Kafkaesque underworlds.

Giving this man an inkling of what has been taken from
him, even in the best possible present circumstances, and of
what immense power still rests within him—this is the theological task. A true theologian is someone who understands
the science of abundance, which transcends mere economy,
and who knows the mystery of the eternal springs, which are
inexhaustible and always at hand. By a theologian we mean
someone who knows—and a knower in this sense is the little prostitute Sonya, who discovers the treasure of being in

Raskolnikov and knows how to raise it to the light for him. The reader senses that these gifts have been brought to the surface not for life alone but also for transcendence. This is the great aspect of this novel, indeed of all of Dostoyevsky's work, which acts like a breakwater on which the errors of the times are pulverized. These are talents that emerge more clearly after every new catastrophe and in which the Russian pen has achieved world status.

25

In the vicinity of the zero meridian, where we still linger, faith no longer has value; here it is evidence that is demanded. One could also say that at this point people have faith in evidence. A rising number of people seem to realize that the spiritual life, even seen from a technical perspective, has more effective forms at its disposal than military discipline, athletic training, or the routines of the work world. Ignatius knew this, and today this knowledge also sustains founders of sects and leaders of small circles whose intentions are difficult to judge—an example is Gurdjieff, from the Caucasus, a remarkable man in many ways.

What instruments should be put in the hands of those who actively strive to leave the wasteland of rationalistic and materialistic systems but are still subject to their dialectic coercion? Their suffering heralds a higher existential state for them. There are methods to strengthen them in this direction, and it is unimportant if these are initially practiced mechanically. The process resembles resuscitation routines for the drowning, which must also first be practiced. Then breathing and a pulse return.

Here the possibility of a new order presents itself. As the Counterreformation corresponded in its essence to the Reformation and was invigorated by it, so we might imagine a spiritual movement that seeks out the terrain of nihilism and places itself in opposition to it, as a mirror image in being. As a missionary speaks to the natives in their language, so it is advisable to proceed with those raised with scientific jargon. Certainly, it becomes evident here that the churches have not kept pace with science. At the same time, some individual sciences are advancing into zones where discussions about core issues become possible.

In this respect a work entitled, say, *A Small Catechism for Atheists*[9] would be desirable. Were a similar undertaking to be erected as an advance outpost by a vigorous spiritual power, it would simultaneously work against the numerous gnostic spirits who strive in this direction. Many differences are simply based on terminology. A spirited atheist always comes across more sympathetically than an indifferent man-of-the-crowd since he concerns himself with the world as a totality. Moreover, such a person is not infrequently open to higher possibilities—which is why the eighteenth-century atheists were truly powerful spirits, and more pleasant than those of the nineteenth century.

26

"Here and now" is the forest rebel's motto—he is the spirit of free and independent action. As we saw, only a small fraction of the mass populace can be counted among this type, and yet these few form a small elite able to resist the automatism, on whom the pure use of force must fail. This is the old freedom in the garments of the new times: the substantial, elemental freedom that awakens in healthy populations when the tyranny of parties or foreign occupiers oppresses the land. It is

9. A play on words and an analogy with Martin Luther's *Small Catechism. Tr.*

not a merely protesting or emigrating freedom, but one set on taking up the fight.

This distinction has an influence on the realm of faith. The forest rebel cannot permit himself the kind of indifference that, like small state neutrality and fortress confinement for political crimes, characterized the past period. The forest passage leads to difficult decisions. The task of the forest rebel is to stake out vis-à-vis the Leviathan the measures of freedom that are to obtain in future ages. He will not get by this opponent with mere ideas.

The resistance of the forest rebel is absolute: he knows no neutrality, no pardon, no fortress confinement. He does not expect the enemy to listen to arguments, let alone act chivalrously. He knows that the death penalty will not be waived for him. The forest rebel comes to learn a new solitude, the kind of solitude that above all the satanically growing malevolence brings with it; its connection with science and mechanics, though this may not represent a new element, does introduce new phenomena into history.

There is no reconciling all this with indifference. In this state of affairs one also cannot afford to wait for the churches, or for spiritual guides and books that might surface. Yet it does have the advantage of leading us beyond mere book knowledge, conditioned sentiments, and inherited beliefs, and onto firmer ground. This effect was already apparent in the difference between the two world wars, at least regarding German youth. After 1918, a strong spiritual current could be observed, which led to an unfolding of talents everywhere. Now it is above all the silence that is conspicuous, particularly the silence of the youth, despite the many extraordinary things they witnessed in the cauldrons and murderous imprisonments of their wartime experience. This silence weighs more than any development of ideas, more even than any works of art. They observed more than just the collapse of the national states. Though this contact with nothingness, even the naked, unadorned nothingness of our century, has been depicted in a row of clinical reports, we should expect it to bear still other fruits.

27

We have repeatedly used the image of man's meeting with himself. Indeed, it is important for anyone intending to undertake a risky venture that he first gain a precise idea of himself. In this the man onboard the ship must take his measure from the man in the forest—that is, the man of civilization, the man involved in the movements and historical phenomena must refer back to his latent supra-temporal essence, which incarnates into history and is transformed within it. A venture of this kind will appeal to strong spirits like the forest rebel. In this process, the mirror image contemplates the primal image, from which it emanates and in which it is inviolable— or, equivalently, the inherited being remembers that which underlies all inheritance.

This is a solitary meeting, and therein lies its fascination; no notary, priest, or dignitary will be in attendance. In this solitude man is sovereign, assuming that he has recognized his true station. He is the Son of the Father, lord of the earth, the issue of a miraculous creation. In such encounters the social element also retreats into the background. As in the most ancient times, man reclaims the priestly and knightly powers for himself. He leaves behind the abstractions, the functions, and work divisions, and places himself in relation to the whole, to the absolute—and a profound happiness lies in this.

Clearly, there will also be no doctors at this meeting. In regard to health, the primal image that each of us carries within is our invulnerable body, created beyond time and its perils, which radiates into its corporeal manifestation and is also a factor in its healing. Powers of creation have a role in every cure.

In the now rare condition of perfect health, man is also aware of this higher form in whose aura he is visibly enclosed. In Homer we still encounter a familiarity with this freshness; it animates his world. We find it associated with a free and open cheerfulness, and the nearer the heroes draw to the gods, so do they gain invulnerability—their bodies become more spiritual.

Today, too, the cure originates in the numinous, and it is important that man allows himself to be guided by it, at least intuitively. It is the patient—and not the doctor—who is sovereign, who provides the cure, which he dispenses from residences that are out of all harm's reach. He is lost only if he loses access to these sources. In his death throes a man often resembles someone astray and in search of something; he will find the exit, whether in this world or another. People have been cured whom the doctors had written off, but none who gave themselves up for dead.

Avoiding doctors, trusting the truth of the body, and keeping an ear open to its voice: this is the best formula for the healthy. This is equally valid for the forest rebel, who must be prepared for situations in which any sickness—aside from the deadly ones—would be a luxury. Whatever opinion one may hold of the world of health plans, insurance, pharmaceutical firms, and specialists, the person who can dispense with all of this is the stronger for it.

A dubious development to be wary of in the highest degree is the constantly increasing influence that the state is beginning to have on health services, usually under philanthropic pretexts. Moreover, given the widespread release of doctors from their doctor-patient confidentiality obligations, a general mistrust is also advisable for consultations; it is impossible to know which statistics one will be included in—also beyond the health sector. All these healthcare enterprises, with poorly paid doctors on salaries, whose treatments are supervised by bureaucracies, should be regarded with suspicion; overnight they can undergo alarming transformations, and not just in the event of war. It is not inconceivable that the flawlessly maintained files will then furnish the documents needed to intern, castrate, or liquidate.

The enormous popularity enjoyed by charlatans and miracle workers today is not only explained by the gullibility of the masses; it also reflects their mistrust of the medical industry and in particular of the manner in which it is becoming automated. However crudely they may ply their trade, these conjurors differ in two important aspects: first, in their treating the patient as a whole; and second, in portraying the cure as miraculous. It is precisely this that a still-healthy instinct seeks, and on which the cure is based.

Needless to say, similar things are also possible in conventional medicine. Anyone who heals participates in a miracle, with, or even despite, his apparatuses and methods, and it is already a step forward if he recognizes this. Wherever a doctor with human substance appears on the scene, the mechanism can be broken, neutralized, or even made useful. Naturally, such direct care is hampered by bureaucracy. Yet, ultimately, it is also true that "on the ship," or even in the galleys where we live, there will always be men who break through the pure functionality, be it through their kindness, their freedom, or their courage in taking direct responsibility. A doctor who does something for a patient against the regulations may, by just such initiative, lend miraculous power to his means. We are truly alive only insofar as we are able to emerge from mere functionality.

The technician counts on single advantages. On a bigger balance sheet things often assume a different aspect. What are the real gains from the world of insurance, vaccinations, meticulous hygiene, and a high life expectancy? It is futile to argue the point, since this world will in any case continue to develop until the ideas on which it is based are exhausted. The ship will sail on, even beyond the catastrophes. Naturally, the catastrophes result in tremendous cullings. When a ship goes down, its dispensary sinks with it. Then other things become more important, such as the ability to survive a few hours in icy water. A regularly vaccinated and sanitized crew, habituated to medication and of high average age, has a lower chance of survival here than a crew that knows nothing of all this. A minimal mortality rate in quiet times is no measure of true health; overnight it can switch into its opposite. It is even possible that it may generate previously unknown contagions. The tissue of the people weakens, becomes more susceptible to attack.

Here the prospect opens up on one of the greatest dangers of our times: overpopulation, as Bouthoul for instance depicted it in his book *A Hundred Million Dead*.[10] Our public health infrastructure is faced with the challenge of containing the same masses whose arising it made possible. But this leads us away from the theme of the forest passage. For anyone contemplating a forest passage, hothouse air is no advantage.

28

It is disquieting how concepts and things often change their aspects from one day to the next and produce quite other results than those expected. It is a sign of anarchy.

10. Gaston Bouthoul (1896–1980), a French sociologist, is considered the pioneer of the study of the sociology of war, for which he coined the term "polemology" after World War II. He argued that overpopulation was one of the driving forces behind war. *Tr.*

Let us take, for example, the rights and freedoms of individuals in relation to authority. Though they are defined in the constitution, we will clearly have to reckon with continual and unfortunately also long-term violations of these rights, be it by the state, by a party that has taken control of the state, a foreign invader, or some combination of these. Moreover, the masses, at least in this country, are barely still able to perceive constitutional violations as such. Once this awareness is lost, it cannot be artificially recuperated.

Violations of rights can also present a semblance of legality, for example when the ruling party achieves a majority sufficient to allow constitutional changes. The majority can simultaneously be in the right and do wrong—simpler minds may not grasp this contradiction. Even during voting it is often difficult to discern where the rights end and the force begins.

The abuses can gradually intensify, eventually emerging as open crimes against certain groups. Anyone who has observed such acts being cheered on by the masses knows that little can be undertaken to oppose them with conventional means. An ethical suicide cannot be expected of everyone, especially not when the suggestion comes from abroad.

In Germany, open resistance to the authorities is, or at least was, particularly difficult, because a certain reverence for the state had survived from the days of the legitimate monarchy; along with its dark sides, this had advantages. Consequently, it was difficult for the individual to understand why, with the arrival of the victorious forces, he was held liable for his lack of resistance, not only generally, as part of a guilty collective, but even personally—for instance, for continuing to practice his profession as a musical director or a civil servant.

Whatever grotesque blooms this accusation may have brought forth, we should not treat it as a curiosity. Rather, it should be recognized as a new trait of our world, and we can only advise that it always be kept in mind in times of widespread public injustice. On the one hand one is suspected of collaborating with occupiers, on the other of being a party lackey. Situations thereby arise in which the individual is trapped between Scylla and Charybdis; he is threatened with liquidation through both involvement and non-involvement.

Great courage is thus expected of the individual; he will be called on to lend an open hand to the law, alone, at his own risk, and even against the power of the state. One may doubt that such people can be found at all. But then they surface and are forest rebels. This human type will step onto the stage of history even against its own will, since there are forms of oppression that leave no alternative. Needless to say, a forest rebel must be fit for the task. Wilhelm Tell also got mixed up in a conflict against his will; but then he proved himself a forest rebel, an individual by whose example the people became aware of their own native power over the oppressor.

It is an extraordinary image: one, or even many individuals making a stand against the Leviathan. Yet it is precisely here that vulnerable spots are revealed in the colossus's armor. It must be recognized that even a tiny group of truly resolved individuals can be dangerous, not just morally but also effectively. In peaceful times this can only be observed in criminals. Incidents in which two or three desperadoes set a whole city quarter in turmoil and cause a long, drawn-out standoff are becoming more frequent. If the relationship is inverted by the authorities becoming the criminals, the defensive actions of law-abiding citizens can trigger incomparably more significant results. The shock Napoleon received from the conspiracy of Malet,[11] a solitary but unrelenting individual, is well known.

11. Claude François de Malet (1754–1812) was a French aristocrat and anti-Bonapartist who in 1812 planned a coup d'état against Napoleon while Napoleon was away on the Russian front. His plan involved announcing

Let us now imagine a city, or a state, in which some, perhaps only a few, truly free men still live. Under these circumstances, a breach of the constitution would be accompanied by high risks. This would support the theory of collective responsibility: the possibility of a violation of rights is directly proportional to the amount of freedom it comes up against. An assault on the inviolability, on the sacredness of the home, would have been impossible in old Iceland in the way it was carried out in 1933, among a million inhabitants of Berlin, as a purely administrative measure. A laudable exception deserves mention here, that of a young social democrat who shot down half a dozen so-called auxiliary policemen at the entrance of his apartment. He still partook of the substance of the old Germanic freedom, which his enemies only celebrated in theory. Naturally, he did not get this from his party's manifesto—and he was certainly also not of the type Léon Bloy describes as running to their lawyer while their mother is being raped.

If we assume that we could have counted on just *one* such person in every street of Berlin, then things would have turned out very differently than they did. Long periods of peace foster certain optical illusions: one is the conviction that the inviolability of the home is grounded in the constitution, which should guarantee it. In reality, it is grounded in the family father, who, sons at his side, fills the doorway with an axe in his hand. This truth, however, is not always visible and should also not be a pretext for objections to the constitution. The old saying holds that "The man is guarantor of his oath, not the oath of the man." This is one ground

Napoleon's death in Paris and very quickly installing a rigorously thought-out provisional government. The plan was largely implemented and failed only when Malet, disguised as a general returned from the Russian front with the news of Napoleon's demise, was recognized and arrested. He was executed along with his fellow conspirators. Napoleon was reportedly particularly incensed by the simple audacity of Malet's plan. *Tr.*

why new legislation meets with so little participation from the people. The apartment story has a healthy ring to it—only we live in times in which one official passes the buck to the other.

The Germans have been reproached, perhaps justifiably, for not opposing the officially sanctioned violence with enough resistance. But they did not yet know the rules of the game, and also felt threatened from other quarters where there was no talk of inviolable rights, neither then nor now. The middle position is always subject to a double threat: it has the advantage, but also the disadvantage, of being both this and that. All the Germans who fell, unarmed and in desperate situations, defending their women and children are to this very day barely considered. Their solitary ends too will be known; their weight will also be thrown onto the balance.

We, on the other hand, must take care that the spectacle of unopposed violence does not repeat.

29

In the event of a foreign invasion, the forest passage presents itself as a possible military tactic. This is true above all for weakly or wholly unarmed states.

As with the churches, so too with armaments the forest rebel does not need to know if or to what degree they have been perfected, nor even if they are present at all. These questions are relevant only on the ship. A forest passage can be realized anywhere, at any time, also against vastly superior forces. In the latter case, it will even be the only possibility of resistance.

The forest rebel is no soldier. He does not know the military life and its discipline. His life is at once freer and harder than the soldierly one. Forest rebels are recruited from the ranks of those resolved to fight for freedom, even when the outlook is hopeless. In the ideal case, their personal freedom coincides with the liberation of their land. This is one of the great advantages of free peoples; the longer a war goes on, the greater its significance.

Also dependent on the forest passage are those individuals for whom other forms of existence have become impossible. An invasion is followed by the imposition of measures that threaten large sections of the population: arrests; searches; registration in lists; forced labor; foreign military service. This drives people to resistance, secretly or even openly.

In this regard a special danger lies in the infiltration of criminal elements. The forest rebel may not fight according to martial law, but neither does he fight like a bandit. Just as little can his form of discipline be called military; this presupposes strong, direct self-leadership.

As far as location is concerned, the forest is everywhere—in the wastelands as much as in the cities, where a forest rebel may hide or live behind the mask of a profession. The forest is in the desert, and the forest is in the bush. The forest is in the fatherland, as in every territory in which resistance can be put into practice. But the forest is above all behind the enemy's own lines, in his backcountry. The forest rebel is not under the spell of the optical illusion that automatically makes any aggressor an enemy of the nation. He is well-acquainted with its forced labor camps, with the hiding places of its oppressed, with its minority groups awaiting their fatal hour. He conducts his little war along the railway tracks and supply routes, he threatens bridges, communication lines, and depots. His presence wears on the enemy's resources, forces them to multiply their posts. The forest rebel takes care of reconnaissance, sabotage, dissemination of information in the population. He disappears into impassable terrain, into anonymity, only to reappear the moment the enemy shows signs of weakness. He propagates constant unrest, provokes nightly panic. He can lay whole armies lame, as happened to the Napoleonic army in Spain.[12]

The forest rebel has no access to powerful means of combat, but he knows how a daring strike can destroy weapons that cost millions. He knows their tactical vulnerabilities, the cracks in their armor, where they are inflammable. He also has a greater liberty than troops to choose his arena, and he will make his moves where greater destruction can be effected with minor effort: at choke points; on vital arteries leading through difficult terrain; at locations distant from the bases. Every advance arrives at extreme points where men and means become precious due to the great length of the supply lines. Every front fighter is supported by another hundred in the rear—and this one comes up against the forest rebel. We are back to our ratio.

The current international situation favors the forest passage; it creates counterbalances that invite free action. Every aggressor in the global civil war must reckon with his back-country becoming troublesome—and each new territory that falls to him increases his backcountry. He is thus forced to intensify his control measures; this in turn leads to a flood of reprisals. His adversary places the highest importance on this erosion and all that may promote it. This means that the forest rebel will be able to rely on a global power, if not for direct

12. Known as the Peninsular War, this seven-year campaign between France's Grand Armeé and the united forces of Spain, Portugal, and the United Kingdom is regarded as one of the first wars of national liberation. It is significant in the present context for the emergence of large-scale guerilla warfare, the disruption of communications and supply lines, and the attacks on isolated French units by partisans, all creating a heavy burden on the French forces. Napoleon called this drain on French resources his "Spanish Ulcer." *Tr.*

support, then for weapons, logistics, and supplies. Not that he
will ever be a party man.

The forest passage conceals a new concept of defense,
which can be put into practice with or without a standing
army. In all countries—but especially in small ones—it will be
recognized that preparing this form of defense is indispensable. Only superpowers can build up and administer grand
arsenals. A forest passage, on the other hand, can be realized
by a small minority, even by a single individual. This is the
answer that freedom can provide—and freedom will have the
last word.

The forest passage has a closer relationship to freedom
than any armaments can; a native will to resistance lives in it.
Thus it is fit only for volunteers, who will defend themselves
under all circumstances, whether a state trains, arms, and calls
on them or not. In this manner they demonstrate—existentially—their freedom. The state cannot boast of an equivalent
consciousness and so drops into a subordinate role, becomes
a satellite.

Freedom is today's great theme; it is this force that will
conquer fear. Freedom is the main subject of study for the
free human being, and this includes the ways in which it can
be effectively represented and manifested in resistance. We
will not go into these details. Fear already diminishes when
an individual is made aware in advance of his role in case of
catastrophe. Catastrophes must be practiced for, as an emer-
gency drill is practiced before embarking on a cruise. An entire
population that prepares itself for a forest passage becomes a
formidable force.

One hears the objection that Germans were not made for
this type of resistance. But there was much that they were not
thought capable of. In regard to equipping with weapons and
communications means, above all with transmitters, in regard

to organizing maneuvers and exercises, to setting up bases and systems adapted to the new form of resistance—in short, in regard to the whole practical side of things, people will always emerge who will occupy themselves with these aspects and give them form. More important is to apply the old maxim that a free man be armed—and not with arms under lock and key in an armory or barracks, but arms kept in his apartment, under his own bed. This will also have repercussions on what are considered fundamental rights.

The gloomiest threat today is that of German armies going into battle against each other. Every increase in the arms buildup on either side heightens the danger. Regardless of, indeed across, these artificial borders, the forest passage is the only path on which common objectives can be followed. Passwords can also be found, exchanged, and circulated to prevent shooting on one another. Training on both sides, even ideological, cannot hurt—it may even be useful to know who will pass to the other side in the fateful moment, as in Leipzig.

A power that focuses on the forest passage shows that it has no intention of an offensive attack. Nonetheless, it can greatly strengthen its defensive capacity, even deterringly so, and at low cost. This would enable long-sighted policies. For those who know their rights and can wait, the fruits fall into their laps on their own.

We want to touch here on the possibility that the forest passage, as a path of mutual acknowledgement between necessity and freedom, could have repercussions on the army by allowing a return into history of the primal forms of resistance from which the military forms emerged. Whenever supreme danger reopens the naked issue of "to be or not to be," freedom is elevated from the merely legalistic sphere to a more sacred plane where fathers, sons, and brothers are reunited. The military model cannot hold its own here. The prospect of empty routine taking over is more dangerous than being unarmed. But this is not a question that concerns the forest passage as such; in the forest passage the individual determines the manner in which he will safeguard freedom. If he decides to serve, the army discipline will be transformed into freedom, will become merely one of its forms, one of its means. A free man gives the weapons their meaning.

30

Like all the estate-based forms, so too the military is being recast with a specialized work character; that is, it too is being converted into a technical function. Of Hercules' labors, it is essentially the first that has been left for the soldier: from time to time he has to clean out the Augean stable of politics. In this occupation it is becoming increasingly difficult to keep clean hands and to conduct war in a manner sufficiently distinguished from the handiwork of the police, on the one hand, and that of the butchers, and even the human flayers, on the other. But this is of less concern to the new commanders than spreading fear at any cost.

In addition, new inventions are driving war into zones where limits no longer exist, and the new weapons have abolished all distinctions between combatants and noncombatants. The premise on which the estate consciousness of the soldier subsists disappears therewith, and the decline of chivalric forms follows hand in hand.

A Bismarck could still decline to act on proposals to bring Napoleon III to trial. As the adversary he did not consider himself authorized for this role. Since then it has become customary to legally prosecute the defeated. The disputes associated with such verdicts are superfluous and without foundation—factions are in no position to judge, they thereby only perpetuate the violence. They also deprive the guilty of the tribunal they deserve.

We live in times in which war and peace are difficult to distinguish from one another. Subtle shadings blur the borders between duty and crime. This can deceive even sharp eyes, because the disorientation of the times, the global guilt, spills over into the individual cases. The situation is aggravated by a lack of genuine sovereigns and by the fact that today's powerful have all risen through the ranks of the factions. The capacity for acts directed at the whole—such initiatives as peace treaties, decrees, festivals, donations, and accretions—is thereby impaired from the start. Instead, the ruling powers intend to live off the whole. They are incapable of adding to or even maintaining it from their own inner surplus: through a gift of being. In this manner the triumphant factions squander the capital to satisfy the pleasures and purposes of the day, as Marwitz had already feared.

The only consolation in this spectacle is its descending movement in a definite direction and with definite goals. Formerly such periods were called interregnums; today they present themselves as our industrial landscapes. They are distinguished by a lack of ultimate validity—and we have already come a long way if we can understand the necessity of this, and why it is in any event better than trying to maintain or reinstall already exhausted elements as valid options. Just as our sensibility objects to the use of gothic forms in the machine world, so it also reacts in the moral sphere.

This has already been treated in detail in our study on the world of work. A person must know the rules of the territory in which they live. On the other hand, the evaluating consciousness remains incorruptible, and this fact is at the root of the pain, at the root of the perception of an unavoidable loss. The sight of a construction lot cannot impart the same quiet contentment that a masterpiece transmits to us, and just as little can the things one beholds there be perfect. Insofar as we know and accept this we are sincere, and such sincerity indicates an appreciation for higher orders of things. The sincerity necessarily creates a vacuum, which becomes apparent for instance in painting and also has its theological counterparts. The awareness of the loss is also expressed in the fact that all assessments of our situation that can be taken seriously relate either to the past or to the future. They lead to either cultural criticism or utopias, if we leave aside the cyclic theories. The falling away of legal and moral bonds is another of literature's great themes; the American novel in particular moves in zones from which the last traces of moral obligation have disappeared. It has reached the naked bedrock, which elsewhere is still covered in decomposing layers of humus.

In the forest passage we are forced to come to terms with crises in which neither law nor custom will remain standing. During these crises, similar patterns to those described at the outset for elections will become apparent. The masses will follow the propaganda, which shifts them into a purely technical relationship with law and morality. Not so the forest rebel. He has a tough decision to make: to reserve the right—at any cost—to judge for himself what he is called upon to support or contribute to. There will be considerable sacrifices, but they will be accompanied by an immediate gain in sovereignty. Naturally, as things stand, only a tiny minority will perceive the gain as such. Dominion, however, can only come from those who have preserved in themselves a knowledge of native human measures and who will not be forced by any superior power to forsake acting humanely. How they achieve this is a question of the resistance, which need not always be exercised openly. To demand as much is a typical idea of non-participants, but in practical terms it would amount to handing over a list of the last men to the tyrant.

When all institutions have become equivocal or even disreputable, and when open prayers are heard even in churches not for the persecuted but for the persecutors, at this point moral responsibility passes into the hands of individuals, or, more accurately, into the hands of any still unbroken individuals.

The forest rebel is the concrete individual, and he acts in the concrete world. He has no need of theories or of laws concocted by some party jurist to know what is right. He descends to the very springs of morality, where the waters are not yet divided and directed into institutional channels. Matters become simple here—assuming something uncorrupted still lives in him. We already saw that the great experience of the forest is the encounter with one's own Self, with one's invulnerable core, with the being that sustains and feeds the individual phenomenon in time. This meeting, which aids so powerfully in both returning to health and banishing fear, is also of highest importance in a moral sense. It conducts us to that strata which underlies all social life and has been common to all since the origins. It leads to *the* person who forms the foundation beneath the individual level, from whom the individuations emanate. At this depth there is not merely community; there is identity. It is this that the symbol of the embrace alludes to. The I recognizes itself in the other, following the age-old wisdom, "Thou art that." This other may be a lover, or it may be a brother, a fellow sufferer, or a defenseless neighbor. By helping in this manner, the I also benefits itself in the eternal. And with this the basic order of the universe is confirmed.

These are facts of experience. Countless people alive today have passed the midpoint of the nihilistic process, the rock-bottom of the maelstrom. They have learned that the mechanism reveals its menacing nature all the more clearly there; man finds himself in the bowels of a great machine devised for his destruction. They have also learned firsthand that all rationalism leads to mechanism, and every mechanism to torture as its logical consequence. In the nineteenth century this had not yet been realized.

Only a miracle can save us from such whirlpools. This miracle has happened, even countless times, when a man stepped out of the lifeless numbers to extend a helping hand to others. This has happened even in prisons, indeed especially there. Whatever the situation, whoever the other, the individual can become this fellow human being—and thereby reveal his native nobility. The origins of aristocracy lay in giving protection, protection from the threat of monsters and demons. This is the hallmark of nobility, and it still shines today in the guard who secretly slips a piece of bread to a prisoner. This cannot be lost, and on this the world subsists. These are the sacrifices on which it rests.

31

As we see, predicaments arise that demand an immediate moral decision, and this is most true where the vortex is deepest and most turbulent.

This has not been, and will not always be the case. Generally speaking, the institutions and the rules associated with them provide navigable terrain; what is legal and moral lies in the wind. Naturally, abuses occur, but there are also courts and police.

This changes when morality is substituted by a subspecies of technology, that is, by propaganda, and the institutions are transformed into weapons of civil war. The decision then falls to the individual, as an either-or, since a third position, neutrality, is excluded. From this point forward, a particular form of infamy lies in non-participation, but also in making judgments from a non-participating position.

The ruling powers, in their changing incarnations, also confront the individual with an either-or. This is the curtain of time, which rises perpetually on the same, ever-recurring spectacle. The figures appearing on the curtain are not the most important point—the either-or facing the individual has a quite different aspect. He is led to the point where a choice must be made between his directly bestowed human nature and the nature of a criminal.

How will the individual stand up to this interrogation? Our future hangs in the balance on just this point. Perhaps it will be decided just where the darkness appears blackest. Alongside the autonomous moral decision, crime forms the other option for preserving sovereignty in the midst of the loss, in the midst of the nihilistic undermining of being. The French existentialists recognized this much correctly. Crime has nothing to do with nihilism; on the contrary, it offers a refuge from nihilism's destructive erosion of self-awareness, a way out of the wastelands to which it leads. Chamfort already said: "L'homme, dans l'état actuel de la société, me paraît plus corrompu par sa raison que par ses passions."[13]

This probably also explains the cult of crime that is so characteristic of our times. Its dimensions and extent are easily underestimated. We get a good idea of its significance by regarding literature with this in mind, and not merely the lower genres, such as cinema and comic books, but also world literature. It would be no exaggeration to say that three quarters of it deals with criminals, with their deeds and their milieu, and that its appeal lies precisely there. This indicates

13. "Man, in the present state of society, seems to me to be more corrupted by his reason than by his passions." Chamfort, *Maxims and Thoughts*. Tr.

how far the law has become dubious. People have a sense of being under foreign occupation, and in this relation the criminal appears a kindred soul. When the bandit Giuliano, a thief and multiple murderer, was hunted down in Sicily, a sense of condolence spread across the land. An experiment in living a free life in the wild had failed; this touched every soul in the gray masses and only strengthened their sense of entrapment. This process leads to a heroizing of wrongdoers. It also creates the ambiguous moral shadow that lies on all resistance movements, and not only on them.

In our present age, each day can bring shocking new manifestations of oppression, slavery, or extermination—whether aimed at specific social groupings or spread over entire regions. Exercising resistance to this is legal, as an assertion of basic human rights, which, in the best cases, are guaranteed in constitutions but which the individual has nevertheless to enforce. Effective forms exist to this end, and those in danger must be prepared and trained to use them; this represents the main theme of a whole new education. Familiarizing those in danger with the idea that resistance is even possible is already enormously important—once that has been understood, even a tiny minority can bring down the mighty but clumsy colossus. This is another image that constantly returns in history and provides its mythical foundations; enduring buildings may then be erected on this base.

It is the natural ambition of the power holder to cast a criminal light on legal resistance and even non-acceptance of its demands, and this aim gives rise to specialized branches in the use of force and the related propaganda. One tactic is to place the common criminal on a higher level than the man who resists their purposes.

In opposing this, it is critical for the forest rebel to clearly differentiate himself from the criminal, not only in his morals, in how he does battle, and in his social relations, but also by keeping these differences alive and strong in his own heart. In a world where the existing legal and constitutional doctrines do not put the necessary tools in his hands, he can only find right within himself. We learn what needs to be defended much sooner from poets and philosophers.

On another occasion we saw how neither the individual nor the masses are able to assert themselves in the elemental world into which we entered in 1914. However, this does not imply that man as a free and individual being will disappear. Rather, he must plumb the depths that lie beneath the surface of his individuality; there he will find means that have been submerged since the wars of religion. He will undoubtedly emerge from these titanic realms adorned with the jewels of a new freedom. But this can only be won by sacrifice, because freedom is precious and may demand that precisely one's individuality, perhaps even one's skin, be offered as a tribute to time. Each individual must know if freedom is more important to them—know whether they value *how* they are more than *that* they are.[14]

The real issue is that the great majority of people do *not* want freedom, are actually afraid of it. One must *be* free in order to become free, because freedom is existence—it is above all a conscious consent to existence, and the desire, perceived as a personal destiny, to manifest it. At this point man is free, and this world filled with oppression and oppressive agents, can only serve to make his freedom visible in all its splendor, just as a great mass of primary rock produces crystals through its high pressure.

---

14. For clarity, the original German reads: "Der Mensch muss wissen, ob ihm die Freiheit schwerer wiegt—ob er sein So-Sein höher als sein Da-Sein schätzt." *Tr.*

This new freedom is the old freedom, is absolute freedom cloaked in the new garments of the times. To lead it to victory, again and again, despite all the wiles of the zeitgeist: this is the meaning of the historical world.

32

It has been noted that the basic sentiment of our epoch is hostile to property, and disposed to intervene in ways that harm not only the concerned parties but also the whole. Before our eyes, fields that sustained owners and tenants for thirty generations are carved up in a manner that leaves everyone hungry; forests that supplied wood for millennia are laid level; and from one day to the next the goose that laid the golden eggs is slaughtered and its flesh used to cook a broth that is shared with all but satisfies none. We had best reconcile ourselves to this spectacle, although large repercussions may be expected from it since it introduces intelligent but rootless new strata into society. In this respect some extraordinary prognoses made be ventured, particularly for England.

On the one hand the attack is ethical, since the old formulation "Property is theft" has in the meantime become a universally recognized platitude. Everyone can have a good conscience regarding a property owner, while the owner himself has long since become uncomfortable in his own skin. Then there are the catastrophes, the wars, the tremendously increased revenues generated by technology. All this not only indicates a living off capital—it leaves no other choice. It is not for nothing that we build missiles that each cost more than a whole princedom once did.

The phenomenon of the dispossessed, the proletariat, has imperceptibly taken on new characteristics. The world fills with new incarnations of suffering: the exiled, the ostracized, the violated, those robbed of their homeland and piece of earth, or brutally cast into the deepest abysses. These are our modern catacombs; and they are not opened by occasionally allowing the dispossessed to vote on how their misery is to be managed by the bureaucracy.

Germany today is rich in the dispossessed and disenfranchised; in this sense it is the richest country on the planet. This is a wealth that may be utilized for better or for worse. Great momentum dwells in any movement supported by the dispossessed; but there is also the danger of it merely leading to a redistribution of injustice. This would be a never-ending spiral. Only those able to climb to a new moral floor in the edifice of the world can elude the spell of pure force.

Alongside new denunciations, a new reading of the old "Property is theft" is in the making. Theories like these are more cutting on the part of the plundered than that of the plunderer, who exploits them to secure his spoils. Long since satiated, he devours his way into new spaces. However, other lessons may also be drawn from our epoch, and the events have certainly not passed without leaving traces. This is true above all for Germany, where the onslaught of images was particularly forceful. It brought profound changes with it. Such changes are only formulated into theories at a later stage; first they act on character. This also holds true for the verdict on property; it separates itself from the theories. As it became evident what property really is, the economic theories passed into second rank.

The Germans were forced to reflect on all this. After their defeat, an attempt was made to impose a permanent dispossession and enslavement on them, a destruction through division. This was an even harder test than the war, but it was passed, silently, without weapons, without friends, without a voice in the world. In those days, months, and years, Germans participated in one of the greatest of experiences. They were thrown back entirely on their own property, on the layer within that lies beyond reach of destruction.

There is a mystery here, and days like these unite a people even more than a critical victory on the battlefield. The wealth of the country resides in its men and women who have endured the kinds of extreme experiences that come around only once in many generations. This lends a certain modesty, but also security. Economic theories may hold "on the ship," but the latent, changeless property lies in the forest, like fertile soil that continually brings forth new harvests.

Property in this sense is existential, attached to its holder and inseparably connected with his being. As the "hidden harmony is stronger than the visible one,"[15] so too is this hidden property our authentic property. Goods and possessions become equivocal when they are not rooted in this level—this much has been made clear. The economic activities may seem directed against property; in reality, they establish who are real owners. This is also a question that is continually asked, and must be continually answered anew.

Anyone who has lived through the burning of a capital or the invasion of an eastern army will never lose a lively mistrust of all that one can possess in life. This is an advantage, for it makes him someone who, if necessary, can leave his house, his farm, his library, without too much regret. He will even discover that this is associated with an act of liberation. Only the person who turns to look back suffers the fate of Lot's wife.

As there will always be natures who overestimate possessions, so there will never be a lack of people who see a cure-all in dispossession. Yet a redistribution of wealth does not increase wealth—rather it increases its consumption, as becomes apparent in any managed forest. The lion's share clearly falls to the bureaucracy, particularly during those divisions where only the encumbrances are left over—of the shared fish only the bones remain.

15. Attributed to Heraclitus. *Tr.*

In this regard it is critical for the dispossessed individual to get beyond the idea of a personal theft perpetrated on him. Otherwise he remains with a trauma, a persisting inner sense of loss, which will later manifest in civil war. The estate has indeed been given away, and there is thus the risk that the disinherited will seek redress in other fields, of which terrorism is among the first to offer itself. Instead, it is better to convince oneself that one will be affected, necessarily and in all cases, albeit for diverse and changing reasons. Seen from the other pole the situation is that of an end sprint in which the runner expends his last reserves in sight of the finish line. In a very similar fashion, the drawing on capital reserves should not be understood as a pure expenditure but rather as investments in necessary new orders, above all in governance on a global scale. We might even say that the expenditures have been, and are such that they point either to ruin or some other extreme possibility.

In any case, these insights cannot be expected of the man on the street. Yet they live in him—the way he comes to terms with destiny and pays the times their toll never ceases to move and astonish.

When the dispossession encounters property as a pure *idea*, slavery is the inevitable result. The last visible property is the body and its working capacity. However, the fears that arise when the mind contemplates such eventualities are exaggerated. Our present terrors more than suffice. Nevertheless, the nightmarish utopias of Orwell and others have their usefulness—even if this particular author showed that he had no idea of the real, immutable power relations of this earth and simply surrendered himself to the terror. Such novels are like intellectual exercises by which a few detours and dead-ends may perhaps be avoided in practice.

By considering the process not from "onboard" but rather from the perspective of the forest passage, we subject it to the court of the sovereign individual. It is up to him to decide what he considers property and how he will defend it. In an epoch like ours, he does best to present as few targets for attack as possible. Therefore, in taking stock of the situation, he must distinguish between things unworthy of sacrifice and those worth fighting for. These are our true, inalienable possessions. They are also that which, as Bias says, we carry with us through life, or, according to Heraclitus, which belong to our particular nature, like a man and his genius. The patria that we carry in our heart is one of these possessions, and it is from here, from the realm of the unextended, that we restitute its integrity when its boundaries are injured in the extended world.

Preserving one's true nature is arduous—and the more so when one is weighed down with goods. There is the danger that threatened Cortez's Spaniards—they were dragged to the ground in that "mournful night" by the burden of gold that they were loath to part with. In comparison, the riches that belong to one's being are not only incomparably more valuable, they are also the very source of all visible riches. Anyone grasping that will also understand that epochs which strive for the equality of all men will bear quite other fruits than those hoped for. They merely remove the fences and bars, the secondary divisions, and in this manner free up space. People are brothers, but they are not equal. The masses will always conceal individuals who by nature, that is, in their being, are rich, noble, kind, happy, or powerful. Abundance will flow their way to the same degree that the deserts grow. This leads to new powers and riches, to new distributions.

To an impartial observer it may also become apparent that a latent, benevolent power is concealed in property, which benefits not only its owner. Man's nature is not only that of creator, it is also that of destroyer, it is his daimonion. When the countless tiny limitations constraining this nature fall, it stands up like an unloosed Gulliver in the land of the Lilliputians. The property consumed in this process is transformed into immediate functional power, and a new generation of overpowering titans arises. But this spectacle too has its limits, its moment in time. It founds no dynasties.

This may explain why regimes are more solidly reestablished after periods in which the call for equality rang throughout the land. Both fear and hope lead the people in this direction. An ineradicable monarchic instinct clings to them, even when their only remaining contact with the figures of kings is at the waxworks. It is incredible how attentive and eager people are whenever a new claim to leadership is brought forward, from wherever or whomever it may come. Great hopes are always associated with any seizure of power, even from the side of the opposition. The subjects will not be disloyal; but they do have a fine sense of whether the powerful are remaining true to themselves and persevering in the role they have given themselves. Nevertheless, the people never lose hope in the arrival of a new Dietrich, a new Augustus—a new ruler, whose mission is announced by a new constellation in the heavens. They sense the veins of golden myth that run beneath the surface of history, directly below the surveyed ground of time.

33

Can the being in man be destroyed? The views differ on this question, not only of confessions but also of religions—it is a question that only faith can answer. Whether this being is conceived as salvation, as the soul, or man's eternal cosmic homeland—it will always be evident that the attacks on it must originate from the darkest abyss. Even in today's world, where the prevailing ideas barely grasp the surface of the process, it is sensed that offensives are underway with other objectives than mere dispossession or liquidation. The charge of "soul mur-der" is born from intuitions like these.[16]

An expression like this could only be coined by an already enfeebled spirit. Anyone with a concept of immortality and the orders based on immortality must find the expression objectionable. Where there is immortality, indeed, where only the belief in it is present, there points may be assumed where violence or any other earthly force cannot reach or damage man, let alone destroy him. The forest is a sanctuary.

The panic so widely observable today is the expression of an emaciated spirit, of a passive nihilism that provokes its active counterpart. Of course, no one is easier to terrorize than the person who believes that everything is over when his fleeting phenomenon is extinguished. The new slaveholders have realized this, and this explains the importance for them of materialistic theories, which serve to shatter the old order during the insurrection and to perpetuate the reign of terror afterward. No bastion is to be left standing where a man may feel unassailable and therefore unafraid.

To oppose this, it is essential to know that every man is immortal and that there is eternal life in him, an unexplored and yet inhabited land, which, though he himself may deny its existence, no timely power can ever take from him. For many,

16. "Soul murder" (*Seelenmord*): a term likely coined by Anselm von Feuerbach, a nineteenth-century German jurist, in his book on the case of Kaspar Hauser, a psychologically traumatized young boy (*Kaspar Hauser: An Account of an Individual Kept in a Dungeon, Separated From all Communication With the World, From Early Childhood to About the Age of Seventeen*, 1932). This popular book was read by the judge Daniel Paul Schreber, whose use of the phrase soul murder in his *Memoirs* (1903) caused it to become well known in psychiatric circles via a classic paper of Sigmund Freud's on Schreber's case, "Psychoanalytic Notes on an Autobiographical Account of a Case of Paranoia (Dementia Paranoides)" (1911). It also formed the topic of an article by Swedish playwright August Strindberg ("Själamord," 1891) commenting on Ibsen's play *Rosmersholm*. Tr.

indeed for most, the access to this life will resemble a well into which rubble and rubbish has been thrown for centuries. Yet, if someone manages to clear it out, they will not only rediscover the spring but also the old images. Man is infinitely wealthier than he suspects. It is a wealth that no one can steal from him, and in the course of time it wells up, again and again, above all when pain has dredged out the depths.

This is what man really wants to know. Here is the germ of his temporal anxiety, the cause of his thirst, which grows in the desert—this desert that is time. The more time dilates, the more conscious and compelling but also empty it becomes in its tiniest fractions, the more will burn the thirst for orders that transcend time.

Man thus dying of thirst looks quite correctly to the theologian to alleviate his suffering, to alleviate it according to the original theological model of the staff striking water from the rock. If today we observe the spirit turning to philosophers for answers to this supreme question and contenting itself with increasingly discounted interpretations of the world, this is not a sign that the foundations have changed but rather that the intermediaries are no longer called behind the curtain. In such circumstances science is a better option, because some of the rubble blocking the approaches is also formed by the grand old words, which first became conventions, then annoyances, and in the end are simply boring.

The words move with the ship; the home of *the Word* is the forest. The Word lies beneath the words like a gold base coat on an early painting. When the Word no longer animates the words, a horrible silence spreads under their deluge—at first in the temples, which are transformed into pretentious tombs, then in the forecourts.

A very significant event here is philosophy's turn from knowledge to language; it brings the spirit back into close contact with a primal phenomenon. This is more important than any physical discovery. The thinker enters a field in which an alliance is finally possible again with the theologian, and with the poet.

34

That new access to the sources may be opened by envoys, by intermediaries—this is one of the great hopes. Whenever a genuine contact with being succeeds at even *one* point, this has powerful effects. History, indeed the possibility of dating time at all, depends on such instances. They represent investitures with primal creative power, which manifests itself in time.

This also becomes apparent in language. Language belongs to man's property, to his nature, his patrimony, and his patria, and it comes to him innocently, without him realizing its bounteousness and wealth. Language is more than a garden whose heirs will be refreshed by its flowers and fruits long into old age; it is also one of the great forms for all goods in general. As light makes the world and its forms visible, so language makes their inner nature comprehensible and is indispensable as a key to their treasures and secrets. Law and dominion begin in the visible and even in the invisible realms with the act of naming. The word is the material of the spirit and as such serves to build the boldest bridges; at the same time it is the supreme instrument of power. All conquests in concrete and conceptual realms, all buildings and all roads, all conflicts and all treaties, are preceded by revelations, plans, and invocations, in word and in language—and the poem leads them all. Two kinds of history can be said to exist: one in the world of things; the other in the world of language. The second contains not only the higher insight but also the more effective power. Even the base must constantly regenerate itself from this force, also when it turns to violence. Yet the suffering passes and is transfigured into poetry.

It is an old error to believe that we can judge when a poet may be awaited by the state of language. Language can be in full decay, and yet a poet will emerge from it like a lion out of the desert. Conversely, fruits do not always follow an exceptional bloom.

Language does not live from its rules, for otherwise grammaticians would rule the world. On the primal ground, the word is no longer form, no longer a key. It becomes identical with being. It becomes creative energy. *That* is the source of its immense, unmintable power. And *there* no more than approaches take place. Language lives and moves around silence, as an oasis forms around a spring. A poem confirms that a man has managed to enter the timeless garden. Time then lives on this.

Even when language has declined to a mere instrument for technicians and bureaucrats and tries to borrow from slang to simulate vitality, in its latent power it remains utterly unweakened. The dullness and the dust merely touch its surface. If we dig deeper, we reach a well-bearing seam in every desert of this earth. And with these waters new fertility rises to the surface.

SUMMARY

(1) The questions put to us are simplified and made more incisive. (2) They drive us to an either-or decision, as revealed in elections. (3) The freedom to say no is systematically excluded. (4) This is intended to demonstrate the superiority of the questioner, and (5) it turns a nay into a venture that only one in a hundred will dare. (6) The arena for this venture is strategically ill-chosen. (7) This is no objection to its ethical

significance. (8) The forest passage is freedom's new answer. (9) Free men are powerful, even in tiny minorities. (10) Our present epoch is poor in great men, but it brings figures to the light. (11) The danger leads to the formation of small elites. (12) The figures of the Worker and the Unknown Soldier are joined by a third, the Forest Rebel. (13) Fear (14) can be conquered by the individual, (15) once he realizes his power. (16) The forest passage, as free action in the face of catastrophe, (17) is independent of the foreground political technicalities and their groupings. (18) It does not contradict the development, (19) but brings freedom into it through the decisions of the individual. (20) In the forest passage there is a meeting of man with himself in his undivided and indestructible substance. (21) This meeting banishes the fear of death. (22) Even the churches can only lend a hand here, (22) since man stands alone in his choices. (23) The theologian may be able to make his situation clear to him (25) but cannot deliver him from it. (26) The forest rebel crosses the null-meridian under his own power. (27) In the questions of healthcare, (28) law, (29) and arms, he takes his own sovereign decisions. (30) Morally, too, he does not act according to any doctrine (31) and reserves the right to judge the law for himself. He takes no part in the cult of crime. (32) He decides what to consider property and how he will defend it. (33) He is aware of the inviolable depths (34) from which the Word rises up to constantly fulfill the world. Here lies the task of being "here and now."

Also from Telos Press

The Adventurous Heart: Figures and Capriccios
Ernst Jünger

On Pain
Ernst Jünger

Hamlet or Hecuba:
The Intrusion of the Time into the Play
Carl Schmitt

Theory of the Partisan
Carl Schmitt

The Nomos *of the Earth*
in the International Law of the Jus Publicum Europaeum
Carl Schmitt

The Non-Philosophy Project:
Essays by François Laruelle
Gabriel Alkon and Boris Gunjevic, eds.

The Democratic Contradictions of Multiculturalism
Jens-Martin Eriksen and Frederik Stjernfelt

A Journal of No Illusions:
Telos, *Paul Piccone, and the Americanization of Critical Theory*
Timothy W. Luke and Ben Agger, eds.

Class Cleansing: The Massacre at Katyn
Victor Zaslavsky

Confronting the Crisis: Writings of Paul Piccone
Paul Piccone